E A M O N
DE VALERA

T. RYLE DWYER

GILL & MACMILLAN

Gill & Macmillan Ltd
Goldenbridge
Dublin 8
with associated companies throughout the world
© T. Ryle Dwyer 1980, 1998
0 7171 2685 4
First published 1980 in the Gill's Irish Lives series
Printed in Malaysia

A catalogue record is available for this book
from the British Library.

1 3 5 4 2

Contents

To Seán, Geraldine, Oonagh, Fiona,
and Malcolm

Preface

Eamon de Valera has been compared with many historical figures such as his own contemporaries Ataturk, Hitler, Franco, Salazar and de Gaulle, or earlier leaders like Napoleon and Abraham Lincoln. He undoubtedly encouraged some of the allusions with Lincoln by keeping a bust of the late American President in his office. Physically they were not too unlike each other: both were tall and thin, with sharp features, and each had come from a modest background. De Valera's first Irish home was a one-room thatched-cottage — the Irish equivalent of the American log cabin. Moreover, each man was deeply involved in his country's civil war.

Many people actually thought that de Valera's involvement in the Irish conflict was in order to prevent partition, just as Lincoln had been primarily interested in preventing the break-up of the United States. But the comparison in that respect was not accurate, because de Valera's prime objective had not been to prevent partition any more than the American President's main aim had been to abolish slavery. Lincoln was quite prepared to support slavery if that would ensure the preservation of the American union. On the other hand, de Valera was ready to accept partition if the nationalist areas of Ireland were granted autonomy and the people there freed from what was symbolically seen as their enslavement under British domination. The motives of the two men were therefore diametrically opposed, with the result that the

comparison of their two careers was rather super-
[2] ficial.

In the same way there were superficial similarities
between de Valera and Ataturk. Both of them shared
an early interest in mathematics, rose to national
prominence as a result of military exploits, and became outspoken advocates of international peace, but
the Turkish leader strenuously devoted his energies
at home to turning his people away from their cultural past, while de Valera sought to do the opposite
with the Irish people. Further allusions could also
be drawn between the Irish leader and the other
prominent people mentioned earlier, but those com-
parisons would again be largely superficial and in
some cases downright frivolous. It was certainly absurd
to contend that de Valera had displayed the military
genius of Napoleon during the Easter Rebellion, or to
compare him with Hitler simply because both of
them could legitimately be classified as revisionists
between the two World Wars.

The famous British leader, David Lloyd George,
concluded that de Valera was unlike anybody he had
ever come across. 'Quite frankly,' he said, 'I have
never found anyone like him; he is perfectly unique.'
He then added rather pointedly that 'the poor dis-
tracted world has a good right to be profoundly
thankful that he is unique.'

De Valera was a leader who frequently inspired
intense loyalty or provoked bitter opposition. He has
already been the subject of several biographies but
most of these have tended to be either uncritical or
unreasonably hostile. The object of this short biography is not to deify de Valera, nor to denigrate his
undoubted accomplishments, but to present an objective picture of him in order that his role in recent
Irish history may be better understood.

Whether people choose to regard his influence as
beneficial or malignant, there can be no doubt that

he has been the outstanding Irish leader of the twentieth century. [3]

This work draws heavily on research for a more extensive project and I would like to thank the people who have helped me in various ways, especially the staff of the Kerry County Library, National Library of Ireland, State Paper Office, the National Archives in both Washington, D.C., and Ottawa, Franklin D. Roosevelt Library in Hyde Park, New York, and the libraries at Marguette University, the University of Wisconsin (Parkside), University of Illinois (Chicago), and both University College and Trinity College, Dublin. I would also like to thank my brother Seán, his wife Geraldine, my aunt Therese Hassett, Tom McEllistrim, T.D., Helen Brassil, Senator Eoin Ryan, Harry Milner, Mrs Virginia Sommers, Mrs F. Kraus, Michael Costello, Fr. Anthony Gaughan, Ger Power, John Lawlor, Joe O'Shea, Paddy Barry, and Declan Keane for their co-operation, help, and hospitality. I should like to thank my mother for reading the MS in all its stages. And finally, I would like to thank Gill & Macmillan for their patience and constructive suggestions.

TRD
Tralee
April 1980

1
The Unifier

On 29 April 1916, after six days of fighting, Commandant Eamon de Valera received an order to surrender. The Easter Rebellion had collapsed the previous day, but communications were so bad that word had been slow to reach him. So he had the distinction of being the last commandant to surrender. As he and his men were being marched as prisoners through the streets of Dublin, he was bitter. The Irish people had proved unworthy of the revolutionaries. Had the people come out 'though armed with hay forks only', he thought that the rebellion might not have failed.[1]

De Valera was certainly an unlikely Irish revolutionary. A married man with four young children, he was the American-born son of a Spanish father. Born in New York City in 1882 he was sent to Bruree, Co. Limerick, to be reared by his mother's family after his father died. Edward, as he was christened, was only two years old at the time. His mother remained in America to remarry and have a second family.

Young de Valera never forgot his first night at the Coll family home — a one-room thatched cottage, which housed himself, his grandmother, two uncles and an aunt. Next day the family moved to a new three-room cottage with a slate roof. One of his uncles and his aunt soon emigrated to America, leaving de Valera, his uncle Pat Coll, and his grandmother to share the labourer's cottage.

At the age of six the boy began attending the

national school in Bruree, where he was known as Eddie Coll. Little Irish history was taught in that school, so he credited the local parish priest* with providing his first introduction to Irish nationalism. Upon finishing his primary education in 1894 de Valera wrote to his aunt in an effort to get her to persuade his mother to arrange for his return to America. He obviously saw little prospect in remaining in Ireland, but nothing ever came of those plans, possibly because the United States was in the grip of a serious economic recession at the time. He did nevertheless manage to persuade his uncle to allow him to attend the Christian Brothers' secondary school in Charleville, some seven miles from his home. He frequently made that long journey to and from school on foot. After sitting his junior grade in 1898, he won a three-year scholarship of £20, which allowed him to continue his education at Blackrock College, Dublin, where he became fascinated with mathematics.

After finishing secondary school, he still had one year of the scholarship remaining, so he enrolled at University College, Blackrock, Co. Dublin. At the time there were very limited opportunities open to Catholics for third level education, seeing that Trinity College, Dublin, was an almost exclusively Protestant institution, and the Royal University of Ireland – the alternative prior to the founding of the National University in 1908 – was strictly an examining institution. The various Roman Catholic colleges scattered throughout Dublin were handicapped in that none of their teachers had anything to do with either the setting or marking of examination papers.

While at University College de Valera was very active in the debating society, where he revealed a distinctly conservative outlook. According to his authorised

*The priest, Fr. Eugene Sheehy, was a granduncle of the historian-politican, Dr. Conor Cruise O'Brien.

biographers, he was frankly committed to one proposition — that a constitutional monarchy was preferable to republicanism. He argued 'that constant elections disturb a nation and are thus not conducive to the prosperity of the people'. In view of the excesses of the French Revolution, he contended that majority rule was a most tyrannical arrangement. In 1902 de Valera received second class honours in his first arts examination and as a result secured a three year scholarship from the Royal University.

The following autumn he took up a teaching post at Rockwell College, where his own studies obviously suffered, as he became deeply involved in the local rugby scene. He played on the senior team and even secured a trial for the Munster team. In 1904 he graduated from the Royal University but, much to his own disappointment, with only a pass degree. He stayed on at Rockwell for a year before deciding to return to Dublin, where he had great difficulty in securing a teaching position. In desperation at one stage he even crossed the Irish Sea for an interview in Liverpool before he eventually obtained a post as professor of mathematics at the Teacher's Training College, at Carysfort, Blackrock.

It was not until 1908 that de Valera first showed any interest in politics or the Gaelic movement. That year he joined the Ard Chraobh (Central Branch) of the Gaelic League and became enthralled with the efforts to revive the Gaelic language. He changed his first name to its Gaelic equivalent, Eamon, and even for a time sought to gaelicise his Spanish surname. In the Gaelic League he made contacts that were to change his life. One of his language instructors was a primary school teacher who was four years older than himself, Sinéad Flanagan, whom he married in 1910. He also came in contact with Eoin Mac Néill, a professor of early Irish history. And when the Irish Volunteers were founded under Mac Néill's leadership in

1913, de Valera was among the first to join.

Like most other people at the time, including Mac Néill himself, de Valera did not know that the Irish Republican Brotherhood (IRB), a secret oath-bound society, was in effective control of the Volunteers and planned to use the organisation to stage a rebellion. He was actually satisfied with the efforts of the Irish Parliamentary Party (IPP) to secure Home Rule from Westminster, but when the British suspended the Home Rule Bill, which was due to become law in 1914, he began to have doubts about the policy of the IPP, especially after the party called on Irishmen to assist the British war effort at the start of the Great War. Had Ireland not been denied Home Rule at the time, de Valera later said that he would 'probably' have joined the thousands of other Irishmen who went to fight on the continent for the rights of small nations. But he stayed at home instead and threw himself enthusiastically into the work of the Volunteers.

In view of the enthusiasm and organisational ability that he displayed, especially within the Gaelic League where he was in close contact with many of the IRB leaders, de Valera rose quickly within the ranks of the Volunteers. He was eventually persuaded to join the IRB, though he never took a very active part in the organisation. As a commandant at the time of the Rebellion he was assigned to hold the area around Boland's Mills, which was on one of the main roads that the British used to rush reinforcements into the city. Men under his command were so strategically deployed that the British suffered very heavy losses trying to use the route.

When the fighting was over it became apparent that de Valera's men had inflicted the heaviest casualties on the British. He was therefore convinced that he would be sentenced to death when he was brought before a military court on 8 May 1916. The other commandants tried before him had been executed, so his wife made representations at the American consulate in Dublin to intercede on behalf of her husband on the grounds that he was an American citizen. Even though the court showed interest in his American birth, he still expected the worst when he was afterwards taken to Kilmainham Jail, where the executions were taking place. As expected he was sentenced to death, but he was surprised to learn next day that his sentence had been commuted to life in prison. What part his American birth played in that decision he did not know, but as another of the commandants, Thomas Ashe — who had no American connection — was also reprieved, along with no fewer than seventy-three others of lower rank, de Valera felt that the British decision had been due to public revulsion over the earlier executions.

Together with more than a thousand others who had taken part in the Rebellion, or who were suspected of sympathising with the rebels, de Valera was deported to Britain. While in jail he won the reputation of being a kind of healing force among the Irish prisoners. For example, one day when some guards were leading Mac Néill into a courtyard, de Valera called the Volunteers to attention and ordered them to salute their Chief of Staff. Though many of the men despised Mac Néill for having tried to prevent the Rebellion, they nevertheless saluted him in the presence of the British guards. Thereafter de Valera was looked upon as a unifier of the Volunteers. He was elected spokesman for the prisoners and he quickly showed the strange blend of leadership qualities that were to distinguish him throughout his years in politics. Robert Brennan, who was a fellow prisoner then, and a life-long supporter afterwards, noted that de Valera was a very good listener in his new role. He actually encouraged debate; yet in the end he would insist on having his own way.

'You can talk about this as much as you like, the

more the better and from every angle,' he would say, according to Brennan. 'In the last analysis, if you [9] don't agree with me, then I quit. You must get someone else to do it.'

From the outside world there were indications that the public odium in which the Volunteers were held following the Rebellion was waning markedly, especially in the United States, where pressure for the release of prisoners was mounting in Irish-American circles. With Britain heavily dependent on American munitions to fight the war on the continent, the London government was deeply anxious to court American favour. Consequently Lloyd George, who took over as Prime Minister in December 1916, announced a Christmas amnesty in which hundreds of Irish Volunteers, who had been interned without even a military trial, were granted an amnesty. These men returned home to reorganise the shattered remnants of their movement.

The metamorphosis that had taken place in the public attitude towards the rebels became apparent in February 1917 when George N. Plunkett, the father of one of the executed leaders, was elected to Westminster in a by-election in Roscommon. He then announced that he would not take his seat but intended to see that Ireland's claim to independence should be heard at the postwar peace conference.

While heartily approving of Plunkett's aims, de Valera had grave misgivings about the Volunteers becoming openly involved in politics, because he was afraid that the movement's momentum could be irreparably damaged by an election defeat. He therefore advocated that the Volunteers 'should abstain *officially* from taking sides in these contests and no candidates should in future be *officially* recognised as standing in our interests or as representing our ideals'. He opposed the idea of putting up one of his prison colleagues as a candidate in the next by-election, but

[10] the man's name was put forward anyway and he was narrowly elected against all the resources of the IPP. Even though de Valera had obviously been slow to appreciate the changes that had taken place in Ireland, he nevertheless showed that he was an astute judge of the international political scene. After the United States entered the war in April 1917 on the pledge of making the world 'safe for democracy', American pressure for the British to do something about the Irish question increased, so Lloyd George announced plans for a Convention in which people representing various shades of Irish opinion would be charged with drawing up a constitution for Ireland. Astutely perceiving that the British government might try to curry favour with public opinion by making the magnanimous gesture of releasing the remaining Irish prisoners, de Valera advocated that the prisoners should engage in a prison strike in order to deprive Britain 'of any credit she may hope to gain from the release'.

They began their campaign on 28 May 1917 by refusing to do prison work, and then when they were confined to their cells, they set about destroying the furnishings. These events were reported in the press and a public meeting to protest against prison conditions was arranged for 10 June 1917 in Dublin. Although the meeting was proclaimed, a sizeable crowd gathered, and there was a confrontation in which a police inspector was killed with a hurley. Against that backdrop the British received little credit for magnanimity when they released the prisoners later that week. It seemed that Lloyd George was simply trying to make a virtue out of necessity.

Having been deported in disgrace little over a year earlier, the men returned to Ireland to a great welcome. De Valera was undoubtedly the hero of the hour, as he was now 'the accepted leader of the men of Easter Week'.

Nevertheless the separatist movement was seriously fragmented at the time. The press erroneously depicted [11] it as being under the control of Sinn Féin — a nationalist political party founded more than a decade earlier by Arthur Griffith — but Plunkett had actually been establishing a rival political organisation, the Liberty League. The whole movement was thus noticeably split when de Valera was invited to run in a parliamentary by-election in East Clare shortly after his release.

From the outset he tried to act as a unifying force. He insisted, for example, that Eoin Mac Néill should be with him as he made his first appearance on an election platform.

Adopting the tactics of a seasoned politician, de Valera remained as vague as possible during the campaign. He endorsed the idea of appealing to the postwar peace conference and the decision not to partake in the Irish Convention, in addition to stressing his own most cherished goal of reviving the Gaelic language. He also emphasised the necessity of not surrendering the rights of the majority to the Unionists in Ulster, but he relied most heavily on an emotional appeal in which he associated himself with the ideals of the executed leaders of the Easter Rebellion. In fact he went so far as to suggest the possibility of again resorting to arms in order to demonstrate his own continuing commitment to those ideals. 'To assert it in arms, were there a fair chance of military success,' he said, 'I would consider a sacred duty.' Yet he avoided becoming too specific about those ideals.

'We want an Irish republic', he explained during the campaign, 'because if Ireland had her freedom, it is, I believe, the most likely form of government.' But he nevertheless emphasised that he was not a doctrinaire republican. He was not firmly attached to any form of government. 'So long as it was an Irish government,' he said, 'I would not put in a word against it.'

De Valera was elected by a comfortable margin of [12] more than two-to-one. He then threw himself into the reorganisation of the separatist movement under the Sinn Féin banner by appearing at public meetings throughout the country. His message was basically the same during the months leading up to the Sinn Féin Ard Fheis (Convention) of October 1917.

He advocated that the postwar peace conference should be called upon to ensure that Ireland got her freedom, but he realised that the country would first need to assert her own nationhood in order to obtain a hearing at the conference. 'To be heard at the Peace Conference,' he told a Dublin gathering on 12 July 1917, 'Ireland must first claim absolute independence'. It was as republicans, he said, that they would have the best chance of enlisting sympathetic support of such countries as the United States and France.

There was actually a difference of opinion between de Valera and Griffith over the most advantageous type of government for Ireland. For years the founder of Sinn Féin had been advocating the establishment of a dual-monarchy on Austro-Hungarian lines. But a few days before the Ard Fheis, de Valera managed to persuade him to accept a compromise formula whereby Sinn Féin would pledge itself to securing a republic and once it had been achieved, the Irish people would then freely choose their own form of government by referendum. He also prevailed upon Griffith to withdraw from the race for the presidency of the party and to propose him instead. At the last moment Plunkett also withdrew, so de Valera was elected unanimously.

He then proceeded to deliver a somewhat confused presidential address. 'This is not the time for discussion on the best forms of government,' he said as he explained that the party was not necessarily irrevocably committed to a republic. 'But we are all united on this — that we want complete and absolute independence. Get that and we will agree to differ afterwards. We do not wish to bind the people to any form of government.' All that seemed moderate enough, but de Valera continued in contradictory terms by declaring that it was 'necessary to be united now to the flag we are going to fight for, that of the Irish Republic. We have nailed that flag to the mast, we shall never lower it.' Nobody was quite sure exactly where he stood. The speech seemed to have something for both moderates and radicals, with the result that the new president was 'hailed as a born leader.'

The following day the Volunteers held a separate convention at which de Valera was elected leader. Consequently he was the head of the most important political and military wings of the separatist movement. The other principal organisation, the IRB, had recently lost its leading figure, Thomas Ashe, the only other surviving commandant of the Easter Rebellion. He had died from injuries received during forced feeding while on hunger strike in jail. De Valera was therefore the undisputed leader of the separatist movement.

He began touring the country as a paid national organiser for Sinn Féin. Calling on the people to repudiate the Convention then sitting, he held out the hope that President Woodrow Wilson's announced war aims would lead to Irish freedom.

With the Allies supposedly fighting for the rights of small nations, de Valera challenged them to name those countries concerned. Once earnest proof had been given that Ireland was to be included among those nations, he promised that half a million Irishmen would be prepared to help the Allies. 'Then they will find,' he said, 'that these half a million men will be ready to defend their own land, and ready to give a helping hand to the oppressed.'

De Valera was deliberately linking the Irish question with the most emotional international issue of the day — the Great War. He explained that the Irish

Volunteers were struggling for the principle of self-[14] determination, so if Wilson was sincere, then they and the Americans were 'genuine "associates" in this war'. The Sinn Féin leader was obviously trying to depict the Irish cause in a favourable light for Americans because, he explained, if Britain ignored Ireland's right to self-determination after the war, he intended to call on the 'great bulk of the Irish in the States' to use their 'weighty influence' to put pressure on the British.

There could be no doubt that he was questioning Wilson's sincerity. 'If President Wilson is honest, he will easily pardon us for not trusting him with an implicit faith', de Valera candidly declared. 'If he is a hypocrite, if he is a meet partner for those who began this world war with altruistic professions of liberty and freedom, then the sooner Americans and the sooner mankind knows it the better.' Yet he emphasised that he was not trying to pronounce any judgment on Wilson. The Irish case, he said, would be the test that 'would prove to the world the sincerity or hypocrisy of the Allies and President Wilson, when they declared that they were fighting for the self-determination of nations'.

De Valera's efforts to bolster Sinn Féin strength initially seemed to make little headway, as the party lost three consecutive by-elections to the IPP in early 1918. The first defeat was in South Armagh, where the Unionist community apparently supported the IPP candidate to the obvious infuriation of de Valera, who afterwards described the Unionists as 'a rock on the road' to Irish freedom and then somewhat recklessly added that 'we must if necessary blast it out of our path.' Within three weeks of making that statement Sinn Féin suffered two further defeats – one in Waterford and the other in East Tyrone, where the Unionists again apparently supported the IPP candidate. It seemed that Sinn Féin was on the wane, but the British soon undermined the IPP by authorising the extension of conscription to Ireland. Members of the IPP withdrew from Westminster in protest, which seemed tantamount to acknowledging that the abstentionist policy of Sinn Féin had been right all along.

The Lord Mayor of Dublin invited representatives of various shades of nationalist opinion to the Mansion House for a conference on what to do about conscription on 18 April 1918. A standing committee was established with de Valera and Griffith representing Sinn Féin, while John Dillon and Joseph Devlin represented the IPP. There was also the mayor, three labour representatives and two independent MPs, William O'Brien and T. M. Healy. The uniformity of opinion that brought such a diverse group of Irishmen together was evidence of the unpopularity of the British measure.

During the Mansion House deliberations de Valera stood out. 'His transparent sincerity, his gentleness and equability captured the hearts of us all,' recalled O'Brien, who noted that the Sinn Féin leader's obstinacy could be 'sometimes trying', but it nevertheless 'became tolerable enough when, with a boyish smile', de Valera would say: 'You will bear with me, won't you? You know I am an old schoolmaster.'

De Valera had a profound influence on the conference, which adopted a declaration that bore the indelible imprint of separatist thinking. Basing the case against conscription not only on 'Ireland's separate and distinct nationhood' but also on the principle that governments 'derive their just powers from the consent of the governed', the declaration denied 'the right of the British government, or any external authority, to impose compulsory service in Ireland against the clearly expressed will of the Irish people.'

At de Valera's suggestion efforts were made to

enlist the support of the Roman Catholic hierarchy, [16] which responded by virtually sanctifying the conference's campaign. The hierarchy directed that mass should be celebrated the following Sunday 'in every church in Ireland to avert the scourge of conscription with which Ireland is now threatened.' It also called on the people to subscribe to an anti-conscription pledge that had been drafted by the Sinn Féin leader.

During the conscription controversy de Valera sought to enlist American support by giving his first ever newspaper interview to a correspondent of the *Christian Science Monitor*. If Britain was really fighting for the principles enunciated by President Wilson, he contended that 'she could apply them without trouble and without delay' in Ireland's case. As things stood the Sinn Féin leader was not prepared to take the chance that the Irish people would be fairly treated, if they dropped their opposition to conscription. 'Ireland cannot afford to gamble,' he said. 'Great powers strong enough to enforce their contracts can safely enter a combination, knowing their strength is a guarantee that the contract will not be violated and that what they stipulated for will not be denied them when success is achieved.' As a small nation Ireland would have no such guarantee.

De Valera also prepared a draft text for a formal appeal to the United States on behalf of the Mansion House Conference. While it was being circulated among the other members of the conference, however, he, Griffith, and several other prominent members of Sinn Féin were arrested for reputed involvement in a supposed German Plot. As the British never produced any convincing evidence that such a plot even existed — much less that they were involved — there was great scepticism about the charges. To most Irish people it seemed that Britain was just taking the Sinn Féin leaders out of circulation because they were proving a political embarrassment. De Valera was certainly not involved in any such plot, but he was deported and spent most of the next nine months in jail, without ever being called for trial.

Sinn Féin tried to make the most of the propaganda potential afforded by the arrests. An edited version of de Valera's appeal to the United States was published in pamphlet form. It ended in mid-sentence, as if he had been arrested with pen in hand while actually drafting the document. By arresting only members of Sinn Féin the British inevitably gave the impression that they thought the party was primarily responsible for organising the widespread opposition to conscription, with the result that Sinn Féin profited most from the popular backlash generated by the issue. The series of election reversals was quickly ended with Griffith's victory in a Cavan by-election the following month.

When the Great War ended in November 1918 de Valera still had high hopes that President Wilson would stand by his lofty wartime pronouncements. The American President had continued to speak in idealistic terms during the final year of the war. '"Self-determination" is not a mere phrase', he declared in February 1918. 'It is an imperative principle of action, which statesmen will henceforth ignore at their peril.'

'If America holds to the principles enunciated by her President during the war she will have a noble place in the history of nations', de Valera wrote to his mother from Lincoln Jail on 28 November 1918. He believed that those Wilsonian principles could be 'the basis of true statecraft – a firm basis that will bear the stress of time – but will the President be able to get them accepted by others whose entry into the war was on motives less unselfish?'

'What an achievement should he succeed in getting established a common law for nations – resting on the will of the nations – making national duels as rare as duels between individual persons are at present: if that be truly his aim,' de Valera continued, 'may God [18] steady his hand.'

Any doubts about the tide of opinion sweeping Ireland since the Easter Rebellion were brushed aside by the results of the general election held on 14 December 1918. Sinn Féin, having clearly indicated in its election manifesto that its representatives would not sit at Westminster but would instead establish their own republican assembly in Ireland, won 73 seats against 26 for the Unionists, and only six for the once powerful IPP, whose leader — John Dillon — was trounced in East Mayo by de Valera, who received almost twice Dillon's support. De Valera's name was also put forward in East Clare, where he was unopposed, and in West Belfast, where he was defeated by Joseph Devlin.

In line with their election manifesto Sinn Féin representatives established their own parliament, Dáil Éireann, in Dublin on 21 January 1919. A Declaration of Independence was adopted and the establishment of the Irish Republic, first proclaimed during the Easter Rebellion, was reaffirmed. The Dáil also voted to appoint de Valera, Griffith, and Plunkett as representatives to the Peace Conference in Paris.

In February 1919 de Valera escaped from Lincoln Jail and returned to Ireland, but he made it clear that his return was only a visit. He intended to go to the United States to drum up support for the Irish cause.

In spite of his incarceration on trumped-up charges, he gave the distinct impression of being moderate in comparison to some of his colleagues. From his hiding place in Dublin, for example, he endorsed Irish-American efforts to enlist the help of President Wilson at Paris. Although some people were already saying that the American leader would not bother trying to get justice for Ireland, de Valera called for patience. 'Pronounce no opinion on President Wilson,' he cautioned. 'It is premature, for he and his friends will bear our country in mind at the crucial hour.'

De Valera was spirited back to Britain to await a ship to the United States, but while he was in hiding the British released the other members of Sinn Féin who were being held for their supposed part in the so-called German Plot. He was therefore free to return to Ireland with the others without being apprehended, so he went back to attend a meeting of the Dáil.

Some of the movement's more militant members planned to stage a great public welcome. An announcement was made on behalf of Sinn Féin that de Valera would be given a civic reception in Dublin. When British authorities proscribed the welcoming demonstrations, it seemed that the party would have to risk a confrontation or suffer a damaging loss of face.

There was some serious soul searching among Sinn Féiners in Dublin. The party executive had not made any announcement about welcoming de Valera, but one of its younger and more energetic members, Michael Collins, explained that he had issued the statement himself under the names of the two secretaries of the party. Speaking 'with much vehemence and emphasis' he made it clear that he was looking for a confrontation. 'Ireland was likely to get more out of a state of general disorder than from a continuance of the situation as it then stood,' Collins explained, according to one of those present. 'The proper people to take decisions of that kind were ready to face the British military, and were resolved to force the issue. And they were not to be deterred by weaklings and cowards.'

On learning of the controversy, however, de Valera asked the party executive to cancel the demonstrations rather than risk a confrontation in which lives might be lost. He was sure that matters of much greater principle would arise in future. 'We who have waited', he wrote to the executive, 'know how to wait. Many a heavy fish is caught even with a fine line if the angler is patient.'

When the Dáil met on 1 April 1919, de Valera was
[20] elected *Príomh Aire* (Prime Minister), and he then
proceeded to name a cabinet that included Griffith,
Plunkett, Mac Néill, Collins, and Cathal Brugha. They
were truly representative of the various factions within
Sinn Féin.

Afterwards the new *Príomh Aire* lost no time in
emphasising that his government's policy would not
be one of blind isolationism. In an interview with a
correspondent of the London *Daily Herald*, he stressed
that Sinn Féin was not an isolationist organisation.
He explained, for instance, that the proper translation
of the name, Sinn Féin, was 'We Ourselves', rather
than the frequently used 'Ourselves Alone', which he
felt indicated isolationism. Instead of 'desiring isola-
tion', de Valera said that the party was dedicated to
getting Ireland 'recognised as an independent unit in a
world-league of nations'.

Soon there were signs that all was not well in Paris.
Speaking in the Dáil on 11 April 1919 the *Príomh
Aire* warned that there were indications that the
League was going to take on the aspects of an organisation designed to preserve the international *status quo*.
It seemed that those at the Peace Conference were
losing sight of the principles Wilson had enunciated.
In particular, de Valera warned that France seemed
bent on imposing vindictive peace terms, with the
result that 'another war of revenge must surely
follow'. While he could sympathise with the French
and understood their attitude, he warned that they
were 'suffering from too many terrible wounds to be
calm at present. It is for those who have suffered less
to compose France and try to save her from an act
that would endanger her future.'

Ireland was ready to play her role in securing a lasting peace, he said. 'We are quite ready to take our
part in a League of Nations which has as its foundation
equality and right among nations.' But if the covenant

of the proposed league were to be lasting, he said that it would 'be based on the principles which occupied [21] ten of the fourteen points of President Wilson – the right of every nation to self-determination. We take up these principles because they are right, and we take them up particularly because the acceptance of these principles will mean that the long fight for Irish liberty is at an end.'

In early May 1919 the draft terms of the Versailles Treaty were published and it became painfully evident that Ireland's claims were going to be ignored. De Valera therefore reverted to what his authorised biographers described as 'his original plan of going to America and of appealing to the people over the head of Woodrow Wilson'.

2

The American Mission

Although de Valera hoped to enlist the popular and financial aid of the United States for the Irish struggle, he was primarily concerned with securing official American recognition. He knew that American officials would be reluctant to recognise the Irish Republic for fear of offending their wartime ally, Britain, but he thought that he might nevertheless achieve the almost impossible by exploiting President Wilson's eloquent pronouncements on democracy and self-determination in order to enlist sufficient popular support to embarrass the American President into helping Ireland.

From the outset, therefore, de Valera viewed his role in the United States as that of propagandist, rather than statesman or diplomat. During his first public appearance in New York, for example, he stated that his aim was to get the public to exert pressure on

President Wilson, 'for this pressure will show him that the people of America want the United States' government to recognise the Republic of Ireland.'

'This is the reason I am eager to spread propaganda in official circles in America,' he added. 'My appeal is to the people. I know that if they can be aroused government action will follow.' He was so conscious of the propaganda angle that he allowed his title to be changed from *Príomh Aire* to President without even consulting the Dáil. The new title obviously afforded a more impressive platform from which to appeal to Americans.

When the controversy arose over American ratification of the Versailles Treaty, de Valera saw it as an opportunity of bringing 'Ireland into international politics' by linking the treaty issue with the question of Irish recognition. Thus he lost no time in denouncing the treaty, but he did so as a supporter rather that a critic of Wilsonian ideals.

For almost six months he concentrated on the treaty controversy as he travelled extensively throughout the United States, speaking to public gatherings in at least thirty states, and making two separate trips from the east to the west coast. In the course of his travels he was careful to speak in terms that appeared consistent with American war aims and at the same time offset what seemed to be the betrayal of those aims at Versailles. He noted, for example, that Ireland's continued subjugation was proof that the principle of self-determination was being ignored even though it had been fundamental to ten of the famous Fourteen Points which had formed the basis of the American war aims enunciated by Wilson.

De Valera wrote privately that his strategy was to let President Wilson 'know that if he goes for his fourteen points as they were and a true League of Nations, Irishmen and men and women of Irish blood will be behind him.'[2] The Irish leader therefore adopted an essentially positive approach by equating the motives of the Irish rebels with those of the Americans who had engaged in the Great War.

'I hold', he said, 'that those of us who were fighting England were in reality fighting for those very principles for which Americans fought.' If he had been an American, he said that he too would have felt obliged to fight in the effort 'to make the world safe for democracy'. Though that noble aim had apparently been betrayed at the Paris Peace Conference, he contended that it was still not too late to achieve it.

'You can do it even now,' de Valera explained in San Francisco. 'If America is determined to champion the cause of democracy in the world, that cause will triumph. If America leads the way towards true democracy, the democracy of England even, and of France and Spain and every country in the world will follow your lead.' He contended that a proper Covenant for the League of Nations could be drawn up in Washington. 'Now is the time to frame it,' he declared. 'It is not enough for you to destroy, you must build.'

The Irish leader centred his case against the Versailles Treaty on Article X of the Covenant of the League of Nations. That controversial article committed League members 'to respect and preserve' the territorial integrity of member states against 'external aggression'. Thus if the United States ratified the treaty while Ireland was still recognised as part of the United Kingdom, Americans would be morally obliged to cut off support to Irish rebels. And in the event that some power intervened militarily on Ireland's behalf — just as France helped the American colonies in their struggle for independence — then the United States would be obliged to help Britain. 'We don't want America, with our own flesh and blood, to be our enemy', de Valera declared as he went on to warn that such an eventuality was possible under the terms

of Article X, because the Irish people were so deter-
[24] mined to secure their freedom that they would fight
anyone getting in their way.

Although de Valera had the reputation of being an
enemy of the League of Nations at this time, he was
not really opposed to the international body itself
nor, indeed, to Article X *per se*. Before the signing of
the Versailles Treaty, for example, he told a New
York press conference that the obnoxious implications
of the controversial article could be rectified if the
imperial nations would 'surrender their colonies and
possessions as mandatories of the League'.

'We recognise,' he explained shortly afterwards,
'that if you are going to have a league of nations, you
must have some article in it like Article X, but it must
be based on just conditions at the start'. The problem
was that Ireland was being dragged into the League as
part of the United Kingdom and unless the United
States made 'an explicit reservation in the case of Ireland', de Valera contended that 'the ratification of
the Covenant by America will mean that England can
hold that America has inferentially decided against
Ireland, has admitted England's claim to Ireland as
part of her possessions, the integrity of which America
must ever more lend her assistance in maintaining.'

When President Wilson set out on a whistle-stop
tour of the United States to drum up public support
for the Versailles Treaty that autumn, he tried to
avoid the Irish question. But he was eventually forced
to deal with it. Explaining that he had not been able
to raise the Irish case at Paris because the talks there
were concerned only with the territory of defeated
nations, he indicated that if the Versailles Treaty
were ratified, the United States would actually be
able to take up Ireland's case at the League under the
terms of Article XI of the Covenant, which, he said,
stipulated that 'every matter that is likely to affect
the peace of the world is everybody's business.'

'In other words,' Wilson added, 'at present we have to mind our own business. Under the Covenant of [25] the League of Nations we can mind other people's business, and anything that affects the peace of the world, whether we are parties to it or not, can, by our delegates, be brought to the attention of mankind.'

De Valera quickly rejected the American President's arguments. 'Instead of relying on Article XI to undo the wrong of Article X, why not set up Article X in such a form that there will be no wrong to be undone?' he asked. 'If President Wilson was not sufficiently influential to get the Irish case before the Peace Conference, working in an unofficial way, he will not be influential enough to get the case of Ireland before the Council of the League of Nations'.

Emulating the American President, de Valera set out on a whistle-stop tour of his own on 1 October 1919. His first stop was in Philadelphia, where he candidly declared that he would accept the Covenant if Ireland were first recognised as an independent country. 'If the Irish Republic is recognised', he said, 'the Covenant will be acceptable.'[3] On the other hand, if the United States were not prepared to grant that prior recognition, then he at least wanted Article X altered so that America would not henceforth be committed to recognise Ireland as an integral part of the United Kingdom. 'Article X is the whole essence of the League,' he told a Denver gathering the following month. 'It is the preserving clause. If you preserve the conditions under which you start, then start right. It is wrong to preserve wrong: This is why we are against the League of Nations.'

Wilson however was unwilling to allow any reservations to Article X or other parts of the Covenant that he thought fundamental, so when the United States' Senate adopted fourteen specific reservations, the President instructed his supporters to defeat the treaty in November 1919. But they then worked to have it

[26] reconsidered, with the result that a further vote was taken in March 1920. This time two more reservations were adopted, and one of those dealt with the Irish question. By a narrow vote the Senate stipulated that in consenting to the treaty it was not only adhering 'to the principle of self-determination' but also renewing a previous expression 'of sympathy with the expectations of the Irish people for a government of their own choice'.

The adoption of that reservation was publicly welcomed by de Valera. 'Our mission has been successful', he announced. 'The principle of self-determination has been formally adopted in an international instrument. Ireland has been given her place among the nations by the greatest nation of them all.' Privately he wrote that the reservation was 'what I had been always wishing for, and it came finally beyond expectations.'[4] But his jubilation was premature, because many of the senators who voted for the reservation had obviously only done so to make the overall treaty so unpalatable for Wilson as to ensure its eventual defeat. Thus when the final vote was taken on the treaty with its sixteen reservations, Wilson's supporters joined with his diehard critics to prevent ratification.

De Valera's overall approach to the League of Nations controversy led to difficulties with the leadership of the influential Irish-American organisation, the Friends of Irish Freedom. Its leaders, Judge Daniel Cohalan of the New York Supreme Court and John Devoy, editor of the *Gaelic American,* were staunch isolationists who resented the Irish leader's suggestion that the United States should renew her efforts to make the world safe for democracy. That kind of talk was sheer Wilsonian internationalism, which was anathema to the judge and Devoy. They had already made it clear to de Valera that they would be opposed to American membership of the League, even if Ireland were admitted to the organisation, so they naturally resented his nationwide efforts to depict 'men and women of Irish blood' as being prepared to support the Versailles Treaty if Wilson would deal with the Irish issue fairly.

Anxious to appear untainted by alien dictation and determined not to share his own leadership role, Cohalan tried to keep the Irish leader out of Irish-American affairs. As a result de Valera's efforts 'to be let into the political steps' that the judge was planning, were rebuffed. The President reported that he was told not to 'go near the political end at all'.[5] But he was not willing to accept that situation.

'The trouble is purely one of personalities', de Valera wrote. 'I cannot feel confidence enough in a certain man to let him have implicit control of tactics here without consultation and agreement with me.' The President was insisting on having the last say on policy formulation, though he was prepared to consult with Irish-American leaders. 'On the ways and means they must be consulted', he wrote, 'but I reserve the right to use my judgment as to whether any means suggested is or is not in conformity with our purpose.[6]

In short, de Valera was insisting on having the final say on tactics to be used by Irish-Americans, while Cohalan did not want him to have any say in those tactics. A clash between them was, therefore, virtually inevitable. In fact, difficulties between them surfaced very quickly.

'I realised early', de Valera wrote, that 'big as this country is it was not big enough to hold the judge and myself'.[7] Irish concerns were obviously of only secondary consideration to Cohalan, who openly admitted that he was primarily interested in keeping the United States out of the League of Nations and weakening Britain's growing influence in America. On the other hand, de Valera wanted Irish considerations to be paramount.

'I desired that Ireland's interest should come first',
[28] he wrote. 'I held that the I[rish] here were organised
not in their own interest here so much as to help Ireland. I held that the money contributed was obtained
in the belief that it would be used as directly as possible for Ireland'.[8]

'It is sympathy for Ireland that has enabled such
an organisation as the Friends of Irish Freedom to be
built up', he wrote on another occasion. 'That is why
the vast mass of the rank and file have joined — that is
why they have contributed, and I will not allow myself to be in any hobble skirts with respect to the
doing of anything which we feel certain is for the
good of the Cause.'[9]

The Friends of Irish Freedom had established an
Irish Victory Fund with the aim of collecting a million dollars, but only a quarter of that was earmarked
for Ireland. De Valera was convinced that he could
collect much more by selling Irish republican bonds.
But Cohalan tried to throw cold water on that project
by pointing out that unless the Irish Republic were
first officially recognised, the sale of such bonds would
be illegal in the United States. The difficulty was
overcome, however, by waiting until the Friends of
Irish Freedom wound up its Victory Fund in August
1919. Then the organisation underwrote a drive to
sell not bonds but bond-certificates that would entitle
purchasers to buy actual bonds of similar value once
the Irish Republic had been officially recognised. By
that subtle arrangement the legal complications were
overcome. Yet the co-operation did little to stem de
Valera's growing disenchantment with the Cohalan
faction. The fault really lay on both sides.

De Valera's own reports to the cabinet in Dublin
left no doubt that he had interfered in American
affairs in the way in which he involved himself in the
controversy over the Versailles Treaty. But, on the
other hand, the Cohalan faction interfered in what

were basically Irish affairs. This became apparent in early 1920 when de Valera tried to undermine the [29] widespread belief that Ireland's independence would gravely threaten Britain's national security.

The President told a correspondent of the *Westminster Gazette* that there were various ways of satisfying Britain's legitimate security needs. He suggested, for example, that Britain could declare a kind of Monroe Doctrine for the British Isles, or even conclude a treaty with Ireland on the lines of the 1901 treaty between the United States and Cuba, whereby the latter guaranteed that she would not permit her independence to be compromised by allowing any foreign power to obtain 'control over any portion' of Cuban territory.

'Why doesn't Britain do with Ireland as the United States did with Cuba?' de Valera asked. 'Why doesn't Britain declare a Monroe Doctrine for the two neighbouring islands? The people of Ireland, so far from objecting, would co-operate with their whole soul.'

The *Gaelic American* took exception to the use of the Cuban parallel on the grounds that the treaty in question included provisions granting the United States not only bases in Cuba but also the right to intervene there in order to ensure the preservation of the island's independence.

De Valera quickly explained that he had only referred to the treaty's provision about maintaining independence and had not been alluding to other aspects of the agreement. Indeed, it should have been apparent from a careful reading of the interview that he was not advocating that bases be granted to Britain. But in spite of his convincing clarification, the *Gaelic American* remained critical of the use of the Cuban analogy. 'When a part of a document is offered in evidence in court, or in negotiations', the editor wrote, 'the whole document becomes subject for consideration.'

Although the President did not attempt to answer this criticism publicly, he did complain to Cohalan about it. In a very candid latter, de Valera explained that he was planning to use 'the great lever of American public opinion' as a wedge to achieve his aims in the United States. And, as the Irish-Americans were to be the thin edge of this metaphorical wedge, he was anxious to satisfy himself that the metal at the point was of the right temper.

'The articles of the *Gaelic American* and certain incidents that have resulted from them, give me grounds for the fear that in a moment of stress the point of the lever would fail me,' de Valera wrote. Consequently, he added that it was vital that he should know how the judge stood in the matter. 'I am led to understand that these articles in the *Gaelic American* have your consent and approval. Is this so?'

Cohalan replied that he had no intention of being used as a lever for alien ends. And he warned that de Valera was making a serious mistake if he thought that other Irish-Americans would allow themselves to be used in such a fashion.

'Do you really think for a moment that any self-respecting American citizen will permit any citizen of another country to interfere, as you suggest, in American affairs?' the judge asked. 'If so, I may assure you that you are woefully out of touch with the spirit of the country in which you are sojourning.'

Cohalan continued, however, in terms that made it clear that he was also taking it upon himself to speak on purely Irish matters when he wrote that accepting 'a British Monroe Doctrine' would be 'utterly at variance with the ideals and traditions of the Irish people'. As a result there could be no doubt that while de Valera had tried to speak for Irish-Americans and was planning to interfere in American affairs, Cohalan was trying to speak for the Irish people and was interfering in their affairs.

When an acrimonious dispute arose between the two men at a New York meeting on 19 March 1920, [31] the Roman Catholic bishop of Buffallo intervened to temporarily settle the dispute on the understanding that henceforth de Valera would not interfere in American matters and the judge would keep out of Irish affairs.

But the Irish leader obviously had no intention of upholding his side of the understanding. Within a week he asked Griffith to get the Dáil to secretly authorise him to spend up to half a million dollars on the upcoming American elections. He was, in effect, hoping to trade Irish-American votes for a commitment from a presidential candidate to recognise the Irish Republic. Believing that 'the only way to play the cards for Ireland' was to secure a firm personal commitment from a candidate in advance, de Valera approached friends of Senator Hiram Johnson, a Republican from California, whom he considered as probably 'the best man available'. But the efforts to secure a firm declaration on the recognition question from the senator were undermined by the *Gaelic American's* gratuitous endorsement of Johnson. Frustrated, de Valera wrote that it was 'disappointing to see a clear nap hand played poorly'.[10]

'Sometimes', he added, 'when I see the strategic position which the Irish here occupy in America, I feel like crying when I realise what could be made of it if there were a real genuine team work *for Ireland alone* being done. As far as politics is concerned, the position is almost everything one could wish for.'

In an effort to exploit the situation de Valera spent the following month trying to enlist the support of southern Democrats, as he toured through the states of the old confederacy. But the tour was a disappointment from a propaganda standpoint. The crowds were small, and there were some hostile demonstrations organised by local branches of the American Legion, which took umbrage at the attitude that Sinn Féin [32] had adopted during the First World War. The Governor of Alabama not only refused to meet the Irish leader but actually stated that he would like to have him deported.

Without large crowds de Valera's shortcomings as a public speaker became more apparent. He had been making a poor impression by reading his speeches in a dull, halting manner but, as there was virtually no voice amplification at the time, that failing had been of little consequence at big public gatherings such as the Fenway Park meeting in Boston, where the size and enthusiasm of the crowd spoke more for the Irish cause than anything he could have said. Even though he had been preceded by much better orators, the *Boston Herald* reported that he was nevertheless effective on the rostrum because he exuded the outstanding qualities of 'passionate sincerity' and 'utmost simplicity' — two characteristics that 'burn their way into the consciousness of everyone who sees and hears him'. That assessment was later echoed in other parts of the country by people like the editor of a St. Louis journal who reported that the Irish President had not tried to pull 'the British Lion's tail out by the roots' at a local meeting. 'There was no grandiosity of oratory, no eloquence, save when the facts presented their own eloquence', the editor noted as he went on to observe that de Valera's 'appeal is not to the emotions at all, but to the mind. He is concerned not simply to state his case, but to prove it.'

The poet, W. B. Yeats, was disappointed in May 1920 when he went to a New York rally at which de Valera impressed him as 'a living argument rather than a living man. All propaganda, no human life, but not bitter, hysterical or unjust. I judged him persistent, being both patient and energetic, but that he will fail through not having enough human life as to judge the human life in others. He will ask too much of everyone and will ask it without charm. He will be pushed aside by others.' [33]

In many respects the famous poet's remarks were prophetic. De Valera did ask too much of some people and they did try to push him aside. But if Yeats thought that the President was going to be a *pushover*, then he was mistaken, as Cohalan and colleagues learned during the Republican Party's national convention in Chicago the following month. They had tried to persuade de Valera to stay away from Chicago, or at least keep a low profile there, but he ignored their pleas and engaged in some blatant campaigning for Irish recognition. His people opened an office across from the convention centre and published a daily newsletter. They also organised a torch-light parade which culminated in the Irish leader addressing some 5,000 marchers. His actions were so blatant that the Chicago *Tribune* published a cartoon with the caption: 'De Valera is not really a candidate at this Convention.'

He was trying to get a recognition plank inserted into the Republican Party's platform in the hope of binding the party's presidential nominee to recognising the Irish Republic, if elected. But the party's resolutions committee rejected the de Valera plank by twelve votes to one.

Afterwards Cohalan managed — by the narrowist of margins — to get a plank accepted calling for 'recognition of the principle that the people of Ireland have a right to determine freely, without dictation from outside, their own governmental institutions and their international relations with other states and people'. But on learning of its acceptance, de Valera objected and demanded that it be withdrawn. The committee's chairman was so annoyed at this foreign interference that he reversed his vote and killed the plank.

As a result Ireland was not even mentioned in the platform. And when de Valera subsequently went to

San Francisco for the Democratic Party's convention, he was again unsuccessful, which prompted critics to observe that had the Republicans adopted a plank, the Democrats would have been tempted to go at least that far. De Valera's public explanation of his reasons for opposing the Cohalan plank in Chicago was a little disingenuous. He contended that he undermined it because it understated Ireland's case. This was supposedly because it merely called for recognition of Ireland's right to self-determination, rather than for actual recognition of the Irish Republic. But Cohalan was justified in doing that if only on the grounds that the Sinn Féin regime had not been set up with the support of a majority of the Irish people. The party did indeed win a clear majority of the Irish seats in the 1918 general election, but it had secured only 47.7 per cent of the overall vote. Moreover, there can be no doubt that de Valera really appreciated the logic of merely calling for recognition of Ireland's right to self-determination. He had actually been following that approach while in Ireland and had endorsed it upon his arrival in the United States. 'Self-determination', he told a doubting Patrick MacCartan, 'is a very good policy.' Indeed he proceeded to emphasise that policy in several of his American addresses. 'What I seek in America,' the President said on more than one occasion, 'is that the United States recognise in Ireland's case Ireland's right to national self-determination, that and nothing more.' Even after his return home he again emphasised the same theme by telling a Swiss correspondent in May 1921 that 'the principle for which we are fighting is the principle of Ireland's right to complete self-determination.'

Obviously, therefore, de Valera had another reason for undermining the Cohalan plank. On one part of his statement regarding the affair he mentioned that it would have been improper for him 'to become a puppet to be manipulated by anyone'. The real explana- tion was probably hidden in that remark. He was apparently afraid that if he did not act, the adoption of the Cohalan plank would create the impression that the judge was in control of the Irish movement in the United States. As things stood the President believed that Cohalan's unsavoury political reputation had turned off many people who thought that the judge was too influential within the Irish movement. So if Cohalan were seen to get the better of things in Chicago, it would certainly have tended to confirm the impression that he was the kingpin of the movement in America.

In a letter to Griffith a few months earlier, de Valera explained that he did not want American politicians to get the idea that the judge was 'the power behind our movement – the man to whom they would have to go. Were I [to] allow myself to appear thus as a puppet, apart from my personal pride, the movement would suffer a severe blow. Those who hold aloof because of the plea that the Judge is running this movement would cry out that they were justified.'[11]

Notwithstanding the setbacks at the two major political conventions, de Valera did not give up hope of using American opinion. In early August 1920 he wrote to the President of the Friends of Irish Freedom calling for a 'a fresh and more vigorous campaign for the enlightenment of the American people'. He proposed that a convention of the Irish race should be held in some central point like Chicago in order to arrange for America's official policy towards Ireland to be made an issue 'definitely, explicitly and above board during the coming election campaign.'

By suggesting Chicago as the site for the convention, however, de Valera was obviously trying to break the stranglehold that Cohalan, Devoy, and their supporters (most of whom were based in the New York area) had on the Friends of Irish Freedom. The organisation's leadership understandably refused to hold a convention before the November elections, but did agree to convene a national council meeting of the organisation in New York on 17 September 1920. In an effort to secure the broadest representation possible de Valera personally telegraphed each council member to attend, with the result that delegates from as far away as California came, but it quickly became apparent that the attempt to re-organise the Friends of Irish Freedom was going to be futile. The Irish leader therefore walked out of the meeting and called on 'all those anxious to help the Irish Republic' to assist in founding a new organisation that would be under the democratic control of members throughout the country, rather than being run by a cabal in New York. He told a meeting next morning, 'We from Ireland simply ask this: that we should be accepted as the interpreters of what the Irish people want.'

The new organisation, the American Association for Recognition of the Irish Republic (AARIR), was formally launched in Washington, D.C. on 16 November 1920. It prospered for some months while the Friends of Irish Freedom suffered serious defections, which not only seemed to justify de Valera's belief that the latter's grassroot support had come mainly from people anxious to help Ireland, but also tended to confirm that Cohalan's prominence had cost the movement support in many quarters. Within a year, for example, the Friends' membership had declined to around 20,000 at the same time that AARIR's soared to a half a million.

De Valera had intended to remain a little longer in the United States but changed his mind following developments in Ireland, where the Black and Tan Terror was entering its most intense phase. In late November Griffith was arrested and Michael Collins took over as acting President. The latter was already looked upon with a certain amount of hostile suspicion by some of his cabinet colleagues because of his brash manner and his interference in matters that had been outside the scope of his duties as either Minister of Finance in the Dáil, or Director of Intelligence in the Irish Republican Army (IRA), as the Irish Volunteers had become known. During August 1920 Collins even took it upon himself to tell an international correspondent that there could 'be no compromise and no negotiations with any British government until Ireland is recognised as an independent republic.' As that statement conflicted with de Valera's more moderate approach of offering to satisfy Britain's legitimate security needs, it seemed that the change of leadership was coming at a most inopportune time, especially as there were indications that Lloyd George had finally begun to turn his attention to the Irish question and was anxious to negotiate. The President threfore decided that it was time to return home to Ireland.

When he sailed from the United States in December 1920, he left behind a viable organisation that was primarily dedicated to serving the Irish cause. His mission was a qualified success. He had secured valuable publicity and had collected over five million dollars, in addition to contributing towards keeping the United States out of the League of Nations, but he had not achieved his primary aim of obtaining American recognition, nor had his efforts to secure the recognition of other countries amounted to anything.

The Soviet Union was the only country that showed any real interest in recognising the Irish Republic. A treaty of recognition was drafted, after discussions with Soviet representatives in Washington, but de Valera was afraid that Bolshevik recognition might damage the Irish cause. He therefore temporised. In fact, he delayed for so long in the matter that Moscow lost interest, but not before he had advanced the Soviet mission in Washington a loan of $20,000. In return he received some jewels as collatoral. The whole transaction was kept a closely guarded secret and was not revealed for almost thirty years, at which time the money was repaid and the jewels returned to the Soviet authorities.

3
Fishing in Troubled Waters

Following his return to Ireland de Valera deliberately tried to portray himself as a moderate by releasing statements, giving written answers to questions submitted by reporters, and in a few instances by granting interviews to correspondents who were spirited to his hiding place. He received a good deal of international publicity and his carefully cultivated image as a moderate was thereby greatly enhanced.

As Lloyd George had been sending out peace feelers indicating that any settlement with Ireland would have to be on the lines of Dominion Home Rule, de Valera showed a keen interest in the whole dominion concept. He left little doubt that the real status of the dominions would be acceptable to Ireland, seeing that even a staunch imperialist like Bonar Law, the leader of the British Conservative Party, had admitted that the dominions had 'the right to decide their own destinies'.

'Thus', de Valera asserted, 'the British dominions have had conceded to them all the rights that Irish Republicans demand. It is obvious that if these rights were not being denied to us we would not be engaged in the present struggle.' He went on to stress that, notwithstanding its name, Sinn Féin was not an isolationist movement. The Dáil had already proved that by advocat- [39] ing that the country should join the League of Nations. 'In fact', he contended, 'we are thoroughly sane and reasonable people, not a coterie of political doctrinaires, or even party politicians, Republican or other.' On the Ulster question the President even indicated that he would be willing to accept a form of partition. 'There is', he announced, 'plenty of room in Ireland for partition, real partition, and plenty of it.' He suggested that the island should be parcelled up into administrative units that would then be associated in a confederation like Switzerland. 'If Belfast – or for that matter, all Carsonia as a unit – were a Swiss canton like Berne, Geneva, or Zurich', he said, 'it would have more control over its own affairs, economic, social, and political, than it is given by the Westminster Partition Act. The real objection to that Act – prescinding from the question of its moral and political validity – is that it does not give Belfast and Ulster enough local liberty and power. In an Irish confederation they ought to get far more.'

On the question of Britain's security, de Valera repeatedly emphasised, as he had been doing since the famous *Westminster Gazette* interview, that the Dáil would be prepared to satisfy Britain's legitimate needs. 'Time after time,' he declared in March 1921, 'we have indicated that if England can show any right with which Ireland's right as a nation would clash, we are willing that these be adjusted by negotiations and treaty.' The following month he explained that after recognising Ireland's independence, Britain could 'issue a warning such as the Monroe Doctrine, that she would regard any attempt by any foreign power to obtain a foothold in Ireland as an act of hostility against herself. In case of a common foe Ireland's manpower would then be available for the defence of the two islands.'

The President was following a carefully conceived
[40] policy. By appearaing moderate he was keeping pressure on the British to negotiate. Although Seán T.
O'Kelly advised that 'the firm stand we take "on an
Irish Republic or nothing" needs not *change* but
development,'[12] de Valera was definitely opposed to
openly adopting such a firm stand.

'There is no use in saying that DÁIL ÉIREANN
cannot negotiate on account of the mandate which is
given it,' the President explained to a colleague. 'That
simply means that Lloyd George will be put in a position of being able to force an Irish Party into existence
to oppose us at the next elections on the platform of
"freedom to negotiate".'[13]

'In public statements', de Valera advocated, 'our
policy should be not to make it easy for Lloyd George
by proclaiming that nothing but so and so will satisfy
us. Our position should be simply that we are insisting on only one right, and that is the right of the people of this country to determine for themselves how
they should be governed. That sounds moderate, but
includes everything and puts Lloyd George, the Labour
Party and others on the defensive, and apologetic as
far as the world is concerned.'

The President's moderate pronouncements were
causing some problems within the revolutionary movement. Both Tom Barry and Ernie O'Malley, two of
the IRA's more active field commanders, recalled in
their memoirs that they were troubled by de Valera's
reputation as a moderate, but each was reassured on
meeting him personally. The President was secretly
advocating a more militant policy. While he did want
the IRA to curtail its normal operations, he actually
proposed that it should engage British forces in a
major confrontation involving some 500 or so men
each month.

To military people like Collins and Richard Mulcahy, the IRA's Chief of Staff, the proposal was absurd,

seeing that the IRA did not have the strength for such operations, but then de Valera did not know much about the organisation's strength. O'Malley was particularly struck by how poorly informed the President seemed to be about the military situation. On mentioning this to Collins and Mulcahy, both of whom had sat in on his meeting with the President, O'Malley found that the two of them were amused. Collins mentioned some of the questions that de Valera had asked and they laughed. O'Malley was uncomfortable. He later wrote that he 'resented their jokes at the expense of the Long Fellow'.

This ridiculing of the President was one of the first signs of a growing rift that would eventually alienate Collins and de Valera. The former had initially been upset when, less than a month after returning from the United States, de Valera had tried to send him to America.

'That Long Whoor won't get rid of me as easy as that', Collins reportedly told one of his men at the time.

Just when de Valera became aware of Collins's attitude is not clear, but he told his biographers that from April 1921 onwards 'Collins did not accept my view of things as he had done before and was inclined to give public expression to his own opinions even when they differed from mine.'

While de Valera was trying to sound moderate in public statements, for example, Collins was being lauded in the *Gaelic American* for standing firm. 'In every instance his utterances sound the same uncompromising note', the New York weekly observed in a report that went on to quote Collins as saying that there was 'only one basis for negotiation, and that is the freedom of our Nation.'

The British actually concluded that there was a power struggle within Sinn Féin in which de Valera was little more than a figurehead, while Collins was

the real leader. They thought that de Valera wanted
[42] peace but Collins was insisting on a military solution.
Lloyd George was anxious to negotiate but he was
afraid of the possible political repercussions. For
talks to be successful, he felt that he would have to
meet with Collins, whom he described as 'the real
head and front' of the Irish movement. 'The question
is whether I can see Michael Collins', the Prime Minis-
said to a confidant. 'No doubt he is the head and
front of the movement. If I could see him, a settlement might be possible. The question is whether the
British people would be willing for us to negotiate
with the head of a band of murderers.'

On 12 May 1921 the British cabinet discussed the
possibility of negotiating with Sinn Féin representatives, but most of the ministers seemed to think that
talking with de Valera would be pointless as they believed that he was only a prisoner of Collins, with
whom they were opposed to negotiating. Nevertheless
the following month while in London for a Commonwealth Conference, Jan Christian Smuts, the South
African Prime Minister, persuaded Lloyd George to
invite de Valera to London for talks.

In the subsequent negotiations, which eventually
led to the signing of the Anglo-Irish Treaty, de
Valera initially played the dominant Irish role before
withdrawing into the background. The negotiations
can be divided into three distinct phases. The first
comprised four meetings in London between de Valera
and Lloyd George during July 1921. The second
phase consisted of a protracted correspondence
between the two leaders during August and September on procedural matters relating to the setting up
of a conference in London, and the final phase was
the actual conference which convened on 11 October
1921 and concluded seven weeks later with the signing of the Anglo-Irish Treaty.

The first of the four meetings between de Valera

and Lloyd George took place on 14 July 1921 at the Prime Minister's official residence in Downing Street. [43] The traditional account of that meeting had de Valera supposedly lecturing Lloyd George on British misrule in Ireland, only reaching the time of Oliver Cromwell by the end of the first session, but the Prime Minister's own record of the proceedings provided a somewhat different picture. He noted that the Irish leader had an agreeable personality and was a very good listener.

During the talks de Valera tried to show as little of his own hand as possible. He wanted the British to make an offer so that the Dáil would then 'be free to consider it without prejudice'. Hence he was prepared to allow the British leader to do most of the talking.

The tactics proved successful. Lloyd George became so frustrated during the first three meetings, which he compared to being on a merry-go-round one horse behind the President and totally unable to catch up, that he put forward specific proposals on 20 July 1921. These offered the twenty-six counties a form of dominion status that was limited by conditions in matters relating to trade and defence.

Next day the President flatly rejected the proposals during his fourth and final meeting with Lloyd George. According to the latter, the Irish leader indicated a willingness to accept 'the status of a dominion *sans phrase* on condition that Northern Ireland would agree to be represented within the all-Ireland parliament. Otherwise, de Valera insisted that the only alternative was for the twenty-six counties to be a republic.'[14]

By offering to accept the 'status of a dominion *sans phrase*', however, de Valera did not really envision accepting dominion status *per se*. This was because he realised that while the dominions were free in practice, they were not in theory. Their freedom rested on their remoteness from Britain, which meant that

Britain was not in fact able to exercise her legal right [44] to interfere in dominion affairs. But if Ireland were accorded dominion status, the British could interfere in Irish affairs at will. Thus de Valera came up with a plan, which became known as External Association. He afterwards explained that the plan was designed to ensure that Ireland would legally have 'a guarantee of the same constitutional rights that Canada and Australia claimed'.

Prior to the conference, which convened in London on 11 October 1921, de Valera formulated only the outline of his plan. In essence it called for Ireland to be outside the British Empire but associated with it in all matters in which the dominions were in fact associated. It was basically a compromise plan. Although he tried to give as little as possible away before the conference, he left no doubt privately that that it was going to be necessary to compromise with the British.

During a secret session of the Dáil on 22 August 1921, for instance, he stunned colleagues by forthrightly expressing his views on the partition question. If Britain were prepared to recognise the Irish Republic, he announced that he 'would be in favour of giving each county power to vote itself out of the Republic if it so wished'. The only other alternative would be to use force on the six counties and he said that he would not be responsible for such a policy. For one thing he did not think that coercion would be successful. And he warned members of the Dáil that if they tried to coerce the North they would be making the same mistake with the majority there that the British had made with the rest of the island.[15]

Next day de Valera went so far as to admit that he was not excluding the possibility of any kind of settlement with Britain. Before allowing his name to go forward for re-election as President, he warned the Dáil that he did not consider that the republican oath bound him to any particular form of government. Rather, he stressed that he saw the oath only as a commitment to do what he thought best for the Irish people. He was insistent that it would not deter him from considering any proposals from the standpoint 'of what I consider the people of Ireland want and what I consider is best from their point of view'.

'I cannot accept office,' he emphasised, 'except on the understanding that no road is barred, that we shall be free to consider every method.' The policy of the cabinet, he added, would be to do what he thought best for the country and 'those who would disagree with me would resign'.

Although most people assumed that the President would lead the Irish delegation to the London Conference, he refused to go for a number of reasons. He told the cabinet that whoever went would have to compromise, so by staying at home he would be able to rally the Irish people to fight for an absolute claim, rather than a compromise, in the event that the fight had to be restarted.

At the time de Valera obviously believed that the conference would end in failure. His talks in London during July had convinced him that the most the British would concede would be a limited form of dominion status to the twenty-six counties and that they would demand, in return, defence concessions and recognition of Northern Ireland's right to partition. 'On both of these', de Valera wrote, 'Lloyd George would be afraid to give way on account of the political opposition his doing so would arouse in England.'[16]

Even if an agreement were reached, the President realised that there would undoubtedly be 'sharp differences' within the Dáil, so he contended that he would be in a much better position to influence radical republicans to accept a compromise agreement than if he were a party to the negotiations himself. In

emphasising that point an allusion was made to what
[46] happened in the United States when Woodrow Wilson
tried to secure ratification of the Versailles Treaty
after being personally involved in the Paris Peace talks.
Moreover, de Valera contended that his staying at
home would afford a tactical advantage because, as he
was head of state and head of the government, the
delegation could always use the necessity of consulting him as an excuse to avoid being forced to make
any hasty decision.

The President proposed that Griffith should head
the Irish delegation with Collins as deputy leader,
but they insisted that he should go himself, so the
issue was put to a vote. W. T. Cosgrave supported
them, while Cathal Brugha, Austin Stack and Robert
Barton sided with de Valera, who had to use his cast-
ing vote to exclude himself.

Griffith then agreed to go, but Collins was very
reluctant. Both Brugha and Stack refused to serve
before he finally relented. Three others were then
chosen 'to work in well' with the two principals.
Barton felt that he was selected for propaganda purposes, seeing that he was both a Protestant and a
member of what had been the landowning Ascendancy
class. The other two, George Gavan Duffy and Eamon
Duggan, were both lawyers, who were included, in
the President's words, as 'mere legal padding'.

When the Dáil was asked to give plenipotentiary
powers to the delegation, one deputy objected. But
de Valera, who had twice previously threatened to
resign as President if the delegation were not given
such powers, was insistent. He said that once a treaty
was signed by the plenipotentiaries, the Dáil would be
free to reject it, if it were not satisfactory. 'Remember
what you are asking them to do', he said. 'You are
asking them to secure by negotiations what we are
totally unable to secure by force of arms.' With that
the motion fizzled out for lack of support.

Nevertheless the cabinet did issue secret instructions stipulating that the plenipotentiaries should
keep in touch with their ministerial colleagues in
Dublin on the progress of the negotiations, should
send a copy of any draft treaty about to be signed,
and should await a reply before actually signing it.
These instructions were issued because de Valera
wanted to keep an eye on Griffith and Collins. He
'felt certain' that they were contemplating a more
moderate settlement than himself, so he thought that
the British government would be more likely to be
induced to do business with them. As he explained
afterwards, he hoped that their tendency to compromise would make them both a 'better bait for
Lloyd George — leading him on and on further in our
direction.' At the same time the President was confi-
dent that he could prevent them from conceding too
much to the British. 'I felt convinced', he wrote, 'that
as matters came to a close we would be able to hold
them from this side from crossing the line.'[17]

In addition to requiring the plenipotentiaries to
report on the progress of the negotiations, de Valera
had a man keeping an eye on the delegation. He had
been instrumental in having Erskine Childers selected
as chief secretary to the Irish side. The President
thought that Childers had influence over his younger
cousin, Barton: they were double first cousins and
Childers had been brought up from an early age by
Barton's parents. De Valera hoped that together, the
two of them 'would be strong and stubborn enough
as a retarding force to any precipitate giving away
by the delegation. . . . I felt that with these in touch
with the delegation, and the cabinet at home hanging
on to their coat-tails everything was safe for the tug-
of-war.'[18]

It did not take Griffith and Collins very long to dis-
cover that they were being used. And realising that
Childers was acting as a kind of spy on them, they

[48] decided to have him excluded from the talks by secretly suggesting to the British that Lloyd George should propose that the leaders of the two sides should meet in a more informal setting than the plenary sessions of the conference.

Lloyd George jumped at the chance of cutting out Childers whom he considered a retarding force on his own efforts to win over Griffith and Collins. The first informal meeting between the leaders of the two delegations therefore took place after the seventh plenary session of the conference on 24 October 1921.

The other members of the Irish delegation did not know that it was actually Griffith and Collins who had asked for the meeting, so they were unaware that it had been their own colleagues, and not the British, who had inspired the rationalisation of the conference, which never again met in plenary session. Instead, there were twenty-four informal sub-conference meetings at which no secretaries were present. Childers was thereby totally excluded from these meetings, while Barton was only invited to four of them — three of which were in the last thirty-six hours before the Treaty was signed.

During the conference the Irish delegation adopted the same basic approach that de Valera had used in his talks with Lloyd George that summer. It offered to agree to External Association in return for a guarantee of Irish unity. Barton noted, however, that the plenipotentiaries did not have a clear picture of what de Valera envisioned with his plan. They had, he said, only 'a hazy conception of what it would be in its final form. What was clear was that it meant that no vestige of British authority would remain in Ireland. The compromise would be as regards our foreign relations.'

The delegation was given a partially completed document, known as Draft Treaty A, in which External Association was outlined, but it was not really supposed to be the draft outline for a treaty, as has been suggested. Instead it was a document designed for diplomatic manoeuvring.

De Valera actually proposed that three draft treaties should be drawn up. Draft Treaty A was simply supposed to be an outline of counter proposals that the Irish side would initially put forward for negotiating purposes. Draft Treaty B, on the other hand, was a propaganda document that would be published representing terms acceptable to the Irish side in the event that the negotiations broke down. De Valera gave Childers and Duffy incomplete copies of those two documents on the eve of their departure for London, but he did not attempt to draw up Draft Treaty S, which was to be the document that the delegation would use as an outline for a contemplated treaty. He explained to Griffith that the delegation would have to be responsible for the further drafting. 'We must depend on your side for the initiative after this', he wrote.[19]

The essentials of External Association were that the British would renounce all rights to interfere in the internal affairs of Ireland and would acknowledge the country's complete independence in domestic matters. At the same time Ireland would agree to be an equal partner with the countries of the British Commonwealth in a kind of 'partial league of nations'.

Instead of the common British citizenship shared by citizens of the dominions, External Association envisioned 'reciprocal citizenship' — the subtle difference being that the Irish people would be Irish citizens, rather than British subjects. Yet they would have the same rights as British subjects while resident in the dominions, and British subjects would have reciprocal rights while in Ireland.

Initially, therefore, de Valera saw no role at all for the British monarchy, but when confronted with the issue in London, Griffith explained that if he were satisfied on all other issues, especially the partition question, he 'could recommend some form of Association with the Crown'.

Assuming that Griffith was actually thinking of allegiance to the British King, the President sought the views of cabinet members in Dublin. All of them – including Kevin O'Higgins, who used to sit in on cabinet meetings – rejected any thought of allegiance.

'We're all here at one,' the President wrote, 'that there can be no question of our asking the Irish people to enter into an arrangement which could make them subject to the Crown, or demand from them allegiance to the British King. If war is the alternative we can only face it, and I think that the sooner the other side is made to realise that the better.'

When Griffith explained that he was thinking of simply recognising the King as head of the External Association to which Ireland would belong, de Valera approved of the idea. In fact, he even persuaded Brugha, who was the most radical member of the cabinet, to give a written undertaking to accept the proposal.

Initially, therefore, de Valera's overall design seemed to be bearing fruit. He was bringing radical cabinet members along with him, while Griffith and Collins seemed to be drawing Lloyd George closer to the Irish position. By promising to agree to a 'free partnership with the other states associated within the British Commonwealth', they had actually persuaded the British leader to try to end partition. Even though the wording of that formula was deliberately vague enough to be in line with External Association, Lloyd George was convinced from his private talks with both Griffith and Collins that they would ultimately agree to dominion status.

It was only with difficulty that Barton, Duffy, and Childers had been keeping the leaders of the delegation in line. They were particularly disturbed that they were not sure what was actually happening in the talks with the British. Duffy and Childers made separate appeals to the President to insist that they should be brought back into the talks, but he refused. The President was really satisfied with the way things were going in London. Writing to Griffith on 9 November 1921 he explained that he had always believed that it would be best if the delegation could manoeuvre the British into the position where any break up of the conference would be on the partition question. 'There is no doubt about it whatever,' he wrote, 'that the delegation has managed to do this admirably.' He went on to advise 'as far as the Crown-Empire connection is concerned, we should not budge a single inch from the point to which the negotiations have now led us.'

In the following weeks Griffith and Collins did argue doggedly for External Association. Using de Valera's basic approach, Collins contended that the plan was essentially a way of ensuring that Ireland would legally have the same status as that actually enjoyed by the dominions. 'It is essential', he emphasised in a memorandum submitted to the British, 'that the present *de facto* position should be recognised *de jure* and that all its implications as regards sovereignty, allegiance, [and] constitutional independence of the government should be acknowledged.'

When Griffith submitted a memorandum arguing on the same lines the following week, Lloyd George cut the ground from under the argument by offering to include in the agreement any phrase which would ensure that Britain's nominal authority in Ireland would be no more in practice than it was in Canada or the other dominions. 'With this offer', Griffith wrote, 'they knocked out my argument'.

The Irish delegation returned home with a British draft treaty for the cabinet to consider on 3 December 1921. Although Griffith was in favour of accept-

ing the document, he had little support from his col-
[52] leagues. There were strong objections to an oath that
was being prescribed for members of the Irish parliament, who would have to swear allegiance to the Irish
constitution and 'to the King as Head of the State
and of the Empire'. Even Collins advocated that the
oath should be rejected.

De Valera criticised the draft treaty on several
grounds. He explained that he could have understood
Griffith being prepared to accept dominion status in
return for national unity, but neither was being
offered. On the one hand, the British terms did provide a somewhat transient recognition of Irish unity,
but they allowed for Northern Ireland to vote itself
out of the Irish Free State, as the country was to be
known. In that event, however, a boundary commission would be set up to redraw the border in line
with the wishes of the inhabitants. On the association
question, on the other hand, the offer of full dominion
status was again somewhat transient because something less than the full freedom of the dominions
would be accorded to the Free State in matters of
trade and defence. Britain was insisting on maintaining specific Irish bases and such other facilities as she
might require in time of war, which would effectively
undermine the country's right to remain neutral in
the event of Britain becoming involved in a war. The
President concluded by advocating that the plenipotentiaries should return to London, try to have
the document amended and, if necessary, face the
consequence of renewed warfare.

Barton suggested that de Valera should return with
the delegation as it was unfair to ask Griffith to break
on the question of the Crown when he was unwilling
to fight on the issue. The President was seriously considering the suggestion when, in response to some
remarks by Brugha, Griffith promised not to sign the
draft treaty.

'I'll tell you what I'll do', the chairman said. 'I'll go back to London. I'll not sign the document, but [53] I'll bring it back and submit it to the Dáil and, if necessary to the people'. De Valera was satisfied with the assurance. He said later that he would 'probably' have gone to London had Griffith not given the undertaking not to sign the proposed treaty.

Shortly before the cabinet meeting broke up, there was a discussion about the type of oath that would be acceptable. De Valera explained: 'If there is an oath at all it should run something like this: I, so and so, swear to obey the Constitution of Ireland and to keep faith with His Britannic Majesty, so and so, in respect of the treaty associating Ireland with the states of the British Commonwealth.'[20]

The President then went on to dictate one or two other forms that he said would be acceptable. Childers asked if in proposing an alternative oath, de Valera still wanted External Association.

The President replied in the affirmative, so Childers was satisfied, but neither Griffith nor Collins heard the exchange. They had thought that the cabinet was satisfied with that aspect of the British draft treaty, which stipulated that Ireland would have the same *de facto* status as the dominions. It was truly extraordinary that there could be confusion on such a point. But the fact that Childers ever asked the question indicated that the President had not taken a definite stand on External Association during the meeting. Yet it was to be the issue on which he would later base his case against the Treaty that was signed ing London less than sixty hours later.

De Valera was in Limerick when he heard by telephone that the Treaty had been signed. 'I never thought they would give in so soon!' he exclaimed on hearing the news. Because of Griffith's undertaking not to sign the draft treaty, he assumed that the British must have agreed to External Association.

'I felt like throwing my hat in the air', the President recalled a few weeks later. He obviously thought his tactics in using Griffith and Collins had been successful and that they were bringing back an acceptable settlement.

4
'That Little Sentimental Thing'

It was only after returning to Dublin on the evening of 6 December 1921 that de Valera learned to his dismay that the Treaty would not only commit Ireland to full membership of the British Commonwealth but would also oblige all members of the Irish parliament to take an oath explicitly sanctioning that connection. The oath, which had actually been proposed by Collins, read:

> I . . . do solemnly swear true faith and allegiance to the Constitution of the Irish Free State as by law established, and that I will be faithful to H. M. King George V, his heirs and successors by law, in virtue of the common citizenship of Ireland with Great Britain and her adherence to and membership of the group of nations forming the British Commonwealth of Nations.

The President's first reaction was to consider demanding the resignations of Griffith, Collins and Barton from the cabinet, but Cosgrave and O'Higgins persuaded him to wait at least until the delegation could explain what had happened in London. He therefore issued a statement to the effect that the plenipotentiaries were being recalled to explain their actions to the cabinet.

At the cabinet meeting, which was held two days

later, Barton explained that he had only signed after being threatened with immediate and terrible war, [55] but he still felt obliged to support the Treaty. As a result, the cabinet accepted it by four votes to three. When the Dáil convened to consider the agreement on 14 December 1921 de Valera immediately divorced himself from the actions of the plenipotentiaries. He accused them of causing a political mess by not referring the Treaty back to the cabinet before signing it. In order to explain the differences that had arisen between the cabinet members in Dublin and the delegation, the President persuaded the Dáil to go into secret session. Although he predicted that they 'probably could dispose of the points of difference in an hour', the Dáil took four days and did not reconvene in public again until the following week.

The records of both the public and private sessions — especially the latter which lay unpublished for more than half a century — provide a valuable insight into de Valera's thinking on the whole controversy, because he spoke repeatedly. It was undoubtedly a measure of the high esteem in which he was held by members of the Dáil that he was allowed to speak so often, seeing that he intervened in the proceedings more than 250 times during the thirteen days of public and private debate.

At the outset of the private session de Valera admitted that the plenipotentiaries had the authority to sign the Treaty. That, after all, had been the purpose of their mission. They had been given plenipotentiary powers by the Dáil, and those superseded the instructions issued by the cabinet, an inferior body. The President declared that 'they could differ from the cabinet if they wanted to, and that in anything of consequence they could take their decision against the decision of the cabinet.'

He had wanted them to take the chance of securing everything by holding out. 'They said at the cabinet

[56] meeting that it was a gamble', he explained to a friend. 'I begged them to risk it. A win meant triumph, definite and final. If we lost, the loss would not be as big as it seemed, for we would be no worse than we had been six months ago.'

De Valera obviously thought that the plenipotentiaries should have taken their lead from him. 'I was captaining a team', he told the Dáil, 'and I felt that the team should have played with me to the last and that I should have got the last chance which I felt would put us over and we might have crossed the bar in my opinion at high tide. They rushed before the tide got to the top and they almost foundered the ship.'

Some critics had great difficulty in understanding the President. His public utterances tended to overemphasise his own republican leanings, so he was unjustly accused of posturing as having been in favour of holding out for a fully independent republican status.

This was important because both Griffith and Collins were justifying their signing of the Treaty on the grounds that there was little difference between what de Valera wanted and what the British were offering. Griffith explained, for example, that he was not prepared to ask the Irish people to go to war 'for that small difference'.

During the private session the President actually made the startling admission that the difference between them had indeed been very small. In fact, he said that he did not believe that Britain would go to war over 'that small difference' or 'that little sentimental thing' as he referred to that extra concession for which he wanted to stand firm.

'I was ready to break if we didn't get it', he said, 'because I felt the distance between the two was so small that the British would not wage war on account of it. You say if it is so small why not take it. But I say, that small difference makes all the difference. This fight has lasted all through the centuries and I [57] would be willing to win that little sentimental thing that would satisfy the aspirations of the country'.[21]

De Valera believed so firmly in his own position that he was willing to explain it in detail. He drew up a draft treaty on the lines of what he wanted, and he submitted it to the Dáil in the hope of getting it substituted for the Treaty.

Document No. 2, as it was called, differed from the Treaty in terms of association, the oath, and defence. In accordance with the President's plan, Ireland would be clearly an autochthonous state – that is a state deriving its powers to govern from its own people rather than from some outside agency like the British parliament, as was to be the case with the Treaty. This was important because if the British parliament had the acknowledged authority to grant powers of self-government to the Irish people, it would also by implication have the authority to amend those same powers. Nevertheless in the President's alternative the Free State would be associated with the British Commonwealth in 'all matters now treated as of common concern' amongst the dominions, and she would have the same privileges as the other dominions, with their respective citizens enjoying reciprocal rights.

The defence clauses of Document No. 2 proposed giving Britain the same bases as the Treaty but stipulated that after five years the British would hand 'over the coastal defence of Ireland to the Irish Government unless some other arrangement for naval defence be agreed upon by both Governments'. This was a significant difference from the Treaty, which stipulated only that the two countries would reconsider the defence provisions in five years.

The only other significant difference between the Treaty and de Valera's alternative was that the latter did not contain an oath. It merely stated that 'for

purposes of the Association, Ireland shall recognise
[58] His Britannic Majesty as head of the Association.'
The clauses relating to the Ulster question, on the
other hand, were virtually identical with the Treaty.
The President explained that 'without recognising the
right of any part of Ireland to be excluded from the
supreme authority of the National Parliament and
Government', Document No. 2 would accept the
actual Treaty clauses concerning Northern Ireland.
In other words, he said, 'we don't recognise the right
of any part of Ireland to secede, still for the sake of
so and so we are willing to accept it.'[22]
During the secret debate he declared that he would
accept the terms regarding Northern Ireland not only
for the sake of 'internal peace', but also in order to
divorce the Ulster question from the overall Anglo-
Irish dispute. 'The difficulty is not the Ulster question'.
de Valera explained. 'As far as we are concerned this
is a fight between Ireland and England. I want to
eliminate the Ulster question out of it.' Consequently
he was ready to agree to the provisions of the Treaty
relating to Ulster even though he found them objectionable from the standpoint that they provided 'an
explicit recognition of the right on the part of Irishmen to secede from Ireland.'[23]
'We will take the same things as agreed on there,'
he told the Dáil. 'Let us not start to fight with Ulster.
Let us accept that, but put in a declaratory phrase
which will safeguard our right.'[24] In short, de Valera
was prepared to accept Northern Ireland's secession
but he was anxious to give the public impression that
he was not formally acknowledging what he was in
fact accepting.
The President realised, however, that it would be
useless trying to get the British government to accept
his proposals by conventional negotiations. 'No politician in England would stand by them', he admitted.
He did not therefore envisage sending a delegation

back to London but intended to present his alternative as 'a sort of appeal to the two nations.' [59]

'It would be a document that would give real peace to the people of Great Britain and Ireland and not the officials,' he said. 'I know it would not be a politician's peace. I know the politician in England who would take it would risk his political future, but it would be a peace between peoples, and would be consistent with the Irish people being full masters of everything within their own shores.'

While de Valera was contending that his alternative was so similar to the Treaty that the British would not fight over the difference, others argued that it was not worth risking renewed warfare on the chance that public opinion would compel Britain to accept Document No. 2. As far as they were concerned it provided little more freedom than the Treaty.

'It is right to say that there will be very little difference in practice between what I call the proposals received and what you will have under what I propose,' de Valera conceded. 'There is very little in practice but there is that big thing that you are consistent and that you recognise yourself as a separate independent state and you associate in an honourable manner with another group.'[25]

In making that admission de Valera was consistent with his earlier views concerning the *de facto* status of the dominions, which he had previously described as complete independence. Since Ireland was supposedly being accorded the same *de facto* status, it should have followed that Ireland would also be completely independent. But, of course, the President did not accept that conclusion. For one thing the country had been compelled to make unprecedented defence concessions, which would in effect deny it the right to remain neutral if Britain became involved in a war. Moreover, he was convinced that Britain would deny Ireland other aspects of complete dominion

freedom because of the closeness of the two islands.
[60] In short, he did not believe that Britain would respect the Treaty.

Griffith argued, on the other hand, that the British would abide by the agreement. 'We think they do mean to keep it,' he said. But even if the critics were right and the British did subsequently violate the Treaty, he was sure that Ireland's position would be stronger than ever. 'They are pledged now before the world, pledged by their signature', he contended, 'and if they depart from it they will be disgraced and we will be stronger in the world's eyes than we are today.'

Collins actually believed that in some respects the Treaty was even better than Document No. 2, especially as the latter did not accord Ireland the protection of dominion status. He felt, for example, that the Treaty's stipulation that the country would have the same status as the dominions would ensure the support and protection of the dominions if Britain sought to infringe on Irish rights, if only because letting such an infringement go unchallenged would set the precedent that Britain had a right to interfere in their own affairs. Even though Collins did admit that the Treaty failed to accord the full independence that he desired, he argued that it did provide the freedom to progress peacefully towards that independence. In short, he saw the Treaty as a stepping stone to complete independence.

Since the President envisioned using public opinion to get the British to accept Document No. 2, it was imperative that his proposals should have general support at home. So when it became apparent that it would not be possible to get anything near that support in the Dáil, he withdrew his alternative and said that he would introduce it publicly at the proper time.

Towards the end of the public debate he did release a somewhat modified version of Document No. 2 to the press, which immediately concluded that the differences between it and the Treaty were not worth fighting over. In fact, the *Freeman's Journal* charged in an emotional editorial that the whole basis for de Valera's opposition to the Treaty was his own vanity. In an obvious allusion to the fact that he was the American-born son of a Spanish father, the editorial added that he had 'not the instinct of the Irishman in his blood' and that the Irish people should 'stand up, and begin their freedom by giving their fate into the hands of their own countrymen.'

De Valera was apparently still rankled by the editorial when he addressed the Dáil the following morning. Though it would be unkind to describe his speech as partly frivolous and largely vain and egotistical, it would certainly not be unjust. In the course of the speech, which took up little over four pages in the official report, he used the personal pronoun 'I' more than one hundred and thirty times.

'Now', he said, 'I have definitely a policy, not some pet scheme of my own, but something that I know from four years' experience in my position – and I have been brought up amongst the Irish people. I was reared in a labourer's cottage here in Ireland.'

The Dáil applauded. This was obviously the President's reply to the snide questioning of his credentials as an Irishman.

'I have not lived solely amongst the intellectuals,' he continued. 'The first fifteen years of my life that formed my character were lived amongst the Irish people down in Limerick; therefore, I know what I am talking about; and whenever I wanted to know what the Irish people wanted I had only to examine my own heart and it told me straight off what the Irish people wanted.'

De Valera then announced that he was resigning as President and submitting the resignation of the whole government. He added, however, that he intended to

stand for re-election and that the Dáil would have 'to
[62] decide before it does further work, who is to be the
Chief Executive Officer'.

'If you elect me and you do it by a majority,' he
declared, 'I will throw out that Treaty.' He would
then offer Document No. 2 'as a genuine peace Treaty
– to the British peoples, not merely Lloyd George
and his government, but to all the States of the British
Commonwealth'.

While de Valera's manoeuvre did win some support, it also provoked a barrage of criticism as he was
accused of trying to get the vote on the Treaty turned
into a personal vote of confidence. Upset by the intensity of the opposition, he withdrew his resignation,
but not before announcing his intention of quitting
politics. 'I am sick and tired of politics', he said. 'So
sick that no matter what happens I would go back to
private life. I have only seen politics within the last
three weeks or a month.'

The Dáil duly voted to accept the Treaty by 64
votes to 57 the following day. The President immediately declared that the vote simply meant that the
majority of the Dáil were recommending the ratification of the agreement but that nothing could be done
to disestablish the Irish Republic without the approval
of the Irish people. The next step would be to submit
the Treaty to the people for ratification. He therefore
called on all those who had voted against the Treaty
to meet the following day. He was obviously marshal-
ling his forces to bring the fight to the people.

Realising the danger of civil unrest, Collins called
for the two sides to take precautions to preserve the
peace. De Valera stood up to respond with his voice
trembling with emotion. 'We have had a glorious
record for four years', he said. 'It has been four years
of magnificent discipline in our nation. The world is
looking at us now – '. At that point he burst into tears
and collapsed sobbing into his chair.

When the Dáil convened again two days later the President formally resigned. He did stand for re-election on a pledge to ignore the Treaty, but he was defeated and replaced by Griffith.

Although out of government, de Valera retained the presidency of Sinn Féin and evidently enjoyed the support of a majority of the party's rank and file. When the organisation held an Ard Fheis in February 1922, for instance, the majority obviously supported a motion that would, in effect, have expelled those who had voted for the Treaty, but de Valera showed himself reluctant to engage in such divisive manoeuvring. Instead, before the motion was put to a formal vote, he secured an adjournment of the convention in return for an agreement from Griffith and Collins to postpone the planned general election until June so that the Free State constitution could be published beforehand in order that the electorate would be better able to evaluate the implications of the Treaty.

In the following weeks, however, the former President made some remarks that gave rise to grave doubts about his willingness to accept the verdict of the people, should it go against him. Speaking in Thurles on St Patrick's Day, for instance, he warned that if the Treaty were accepted it would mean that the Volunteers of the future would have to fight their own fellow-countrymen, if they should try to complete the work of the past five years. They would, he said, have 'to wade through Irish blood, through the blood of the soldiers of the Irish government, and through, perhaps, the blood of some members of the government in order to get Irish freedom'.

Taken in their proper context the remarks were merely an assessment of the danger facing the Irish people, but critics interpreted them as threatening civil war. They felt he was, in effect, warning that there would be civil strife if the Treaty were ratified, and their fears were exacerbated a couple of days later when he made the aphoristic statement that 'the people have never a right to do wrong'. De Valera 'was not necessarily responsible for what fools or knaves might read into his words', one of his earlier biographers aptly wrote, 'but he certainly gave knaves and fools most ample opportunities'.

Less than a week later, for example, many people looked on the former President as the instigator when Rory O'Connor, the IRA's director of engineering, announced that certain elements of the army were determined to take matters into their own hands, regardless of the wishes of the people. O'Connor made it clear that these dissident elements were not only repudiating their own pro-Treaty leadership but also withdrawing their allegiance from the Dáil. In fact, he indicated that they were prepared to establish a military dictatorship. These dissidents effectively split the IRA by holding their own convention in late March and electing a new sixteen-man executive. Under that new leadership they began to adopt a more militant approach that included bank robberies, raids for arms, disrupting public meetings, wrecking the machinery of the *Freeman's Journal*, and occupying some prominent Dublin buildings — among them the Four Courts, which they used as their headquarters.

While de Valera personally disagreed with their actions — especially their repudiation of the Dáil, he was not prepared to openly criticise them because he was anxious 'to avoid the appearance of a split' in the anti-Treaty ranks.[26] If he were to have any hope of turning them back in the right direction, it was imperative that he should avoid such a split. He did acknowledge 'the will of the Irish people as supreme', but in his efforts to preserve the united front he also made remarks that had all the appearance of encouraging the drift towards anarchy. In an emotional Easter message, for example, he called on the young people of Ireland to act, as their goal was at last in sight. 'Ireland is yours for the taking', he declared. [65]

With public meetings being frequently disrupted — sometimes by actual gun play — it seemed likely that there would be massive intimidation at the polls. Griffith and Collins therefore sought to enlist de Valera's help to prevent such tactics, but he refused. Instead he suggested that the election should be delayed for a further six months in order to allow 'the present passions to subside, for personalities to disappear, and the fundamental differences between the two sides to be appreciated'. In short, he realised that the three months delay had not been sufficient so he wanted a further postponment of the election because he knew that his own views would otherwise be rejected by the majority.

There were understandable reasons for refusing to use his influence to prevent republican intimidation, but he made a deplorable blunder in issuing a statement to the press justifying his refusal on the grounds that there were 'rights which a minority may justly uphold, even by arms, against a majority'.[27] He could so easily have based his refusal on the more rational grounds that his opponents were really using Lloyd George's threat of terrible war as a means of actually intimidating people into supporting the Treaty.

'We know the Irish people do not want to forswear the independence which they have declared', he told an American correspondent a fortnight later. 'We know that they do not want to abandon their distinct nationality, or exchange the title of Irish citizen for that of British subject. We know they do not want a British King as King of Ireland, nor do they want to owe an allegiance which they will never render, but the threat of immediate and terrible war is being used to intimidate them into a false position.' In all probability he was right; the Irish people were being intimidated into supporting the Treaty by the threat of war.

It came to most people as a tremendous surprise
[66] when it was announced on 20 May 1922 that de
Valera and Collins had come to an agreement that
would ostensibly take the Treaty issue out of the
election and thus allow for balloting without the
anticipated intimidation. They had agreed that the
two wings of Sinn Féin would put up a united panel
of candidates in proportion to their existing strength
in the Dáil, and that if elected, the party would form
a kind of coalition government with portfolios being
allocated to the two wings in proportion to the pre-
election strength of each. The adjourned Ard Fheis
was reconvened, and it ratified the pact.

Although de Valera scrupulously kept his side of
the agreement, Collins appeared to violate its spirit –
if not its actual letter – at the eleventh hour by calling on the people of Cork to vote for the candidates
they thought best, instead of only for those on the
Sinn Féin panel. In addition, the pro-Treaty people
also seemed to violate the spirit of the earlier agreement to publish the Free State constitution before
the election so that the electorate could evaluate its
implications. They did release the constitution before
the election but so late that the first chance the people had to examine it was in the morning newspapers
on polling day.

In spite of all that, and coupled with the fact that
the voting register was out of date with the franchise
thus being denied to some young people – who might
have been expected to support anti-Treaty candidates
– there really could be no doubt that the overwhelming majority of the people supported the Treaty. Pro-
Treaty candidates actually polled over 78 per cent of
first-preference votes, while anti-Treaty people received less than 22 per cent. De Valera himself admitted to a friend that 'the decision of the majority
of the people' had 'undoubtedly' gone against the
Republicans.[28]

5
From behind a Glass Wall

Following the general election of June 1922 the anti-Treaty IRA held another convention at which it was proposed that the truce with Britain should be terminated and an attack made on British forces still remaining in the country. Twelve of the sixteen-man executive supported the motion but it was opposed by the Chief of Staff, Liam Lynch, and narrowly rejected. Refusing to accept the decision, the dissidents repudiated Lynch and withdrew to the Four Courts, where only those who supported the motion were admitted. They then elected a new Chief of Staff of their own, thereby splitting even the anti-Treaty IRA. But the split was soon healed when pro-Treaty forces attacked the Four Courts on 28 June 1922. Men like de Valera, who personally deplored the behaviour of those in the building, quickly rallied to them. 'They are the best and bravest of our nation, and would most loyally have obeyed the will of the Irish people freely expressed, but are not willing that Ireland's independence should be abandoned under the lash of an alien government', he told the press on the day of the attack.

Since the Colonial Secretary, Winston Churchill, had told the House of Commons only hours earlier that the British government would consider the Treaty violated if the Four Courts were not cleared out without delay, de Valera contended that the pro-Treaty people were doing the bidding of the British. He was particularly annoyed that no effort had been made to seek authority for the attack from either the second Dáil, which was due to meet in two days in order to formally dissolve, or from the third Dáil which was scheduled to convene the day after that.

Indeed the former President later contended that the pro-Treaty faction had engaged in 'an Executive *coup d'état'*, seeing that the Dáil was ignored in that whole crisis which provided the spark that ignited the Civil War. The second Dáil never did formally dissolve, and the opening session of the third was postponed on several different occasions and did not meet until September, by which time Cosgrave had taken over the leadership of the pro-Treaty side in succession to Griffith and Collins, both of whom were dead.

De Valera endorsed a decision calling on Republican deputies to abstain from the Dáil, but he was reluctant to go along with a plan to establish a separate assembly and claim it as the legitimate parliament of the Republic. He explained that the resulting government would have no chance of securing the allegiance of even the anti-Treaty IRA, with the result that it 'would only be a farce'.[29]

Though de Valera was frequently accused of being the mastermind of the Republican campaign, he really had little say in military matters. In fact, after the fighting began he enlisted in the IRA as a mere private. He did remain as leader of the political wing of the movement, but the IRA's repudiation of the Dáil had, in effect, been a repudiation of all political control, with the result that de Valera and the other anti-Treaty politicians had little real influence with the gunmen.

'The present position is', he wrote in September 1922, 'that we have all the public responsibility, and no voice and no authority.' He actually considered calling on his political colleagues to resign their positions in order to clarify the situation. 'This is the course I have been tempted to take myself', he explained, 'and were it not that my action might prejudice the cause of the Republic, I'd have taken it long since. Our position as public representatives is impossible.'[30] Nevertheless he allowed himself to be drafted as President of a rebel government the following month.

The Republicans argued that as the second Dáil had never formally dissolved, it was therefore in existence. Consequently its anti-Treaty members met and requested de Valera to resume the presidency. But his correspondence during the following months clearly showed that his supposed government had not secured that necessary 'unconditional allegiance' of the army without which he had himself said it 'would only be a farce'.

When he tried to influence the army, he seemed to have little impact. For example, he objected to the IRA's tactic of burning the homes of members of the Free State Dáil. In one such fire in December 1922 the young son of one deputy lost his life, so de Valera protested against such acts on the grounds that these looked like reprisals against the families of opponents. 'Terroristic methods may silence those of our opponents who are cowards,' he wrote, 'but many of them are very far from being cowards, and attempts at terrorism will only stiffen the bold men amongst them. I am against such methods on principle, and believe we will never win in this war unless we attach the people to our government by contrast with theirs.'

Little heed was paid to that advice. The IRA actually began taking deliberate reprisals against the families of prominent Free State officials — the more notable of which were the murders of an uncle of President Cosgrave and the father of Vice-President O'Higgins. On the other hand, Free State troops later descended to the depths of depravity by torturing prisoners and then killing them in a heinous manner, such as at Ballyseedy Cross, near Tralee, where nine prisoners were tied to the stump of a tree in which a mine had been placed. It was then detonated, killing eight of the men. By some explosive freak one of the prisoners managed to escape, as did another man in a comparatively similar incident near Killarney that same day. But when Free State troops used those tactics to kill five more men near Cahirciveen the following week, they took the barbarous precaution of first shooting each man in the legs to make sure that he could not escape. Incidents like those were responsible for the intensity of the bitterness that was to pervade Irish politics for many years.

Unable to influence the course of events de Valera watched in impotent frustration. 'I have been condemned,' he wrote, 'to view the tragedy here for the last year as through a wall of glass, powerless to intervene effectively.' He did try to exert a moderating influence by suggesting that the acceptance of Document No. 2 offered the best avenue to peace, but his suggestion provoked a rebuke from Lynch, who obviously felt that the IRA should be seen to be fighting for more than that 'little sentimental' difference between the Treaty and Document No. 2.

De Valera was furious. 'I will take no further responsibility for publicly handling the situation,' he wrote to Lynch, 'if I have, at every turn, to account for what I say, to people who have not given a moment's thought to the whole question.' He added that many people had come to the conclusion that the IRA was beaten and he would certainly agree with them if the struggle was for an 'isolated Republic'.

That caustic response seemed to betray de Valera's irritation at the way things were going and his own inability to influence events. Shortly afterwards he showed similar frustration at the hardline views being expressed by another of the more radical Republicans, Mary MacSwiney. In one letter to her, he explained that he tended to overestimate the strength of the Free State army and underestimate that of the IRA, while she tended to do the opposite in both cases. Continuing with insulting frankness he wrote that 'of the two I have no doubt that an omniscient being would rate my error as but a very small fraction of yours — vanity?' [71]

In late March 1923 de Valera made strenuous efforts to persuade the IRA to seek peace, but when he tried to attend a secret meeting of the executive in the Waterford mountains, he was kept waiting for some time as those inside debated whether or not to even admit him. And when he did finally get in, it was made clear that he would have no vote. He supported a motion calling on the army to suspend its activities and call off its campaign, but Lynch, who still retained the hope of defeating the Free State forces, managed to persuade his colleagues to defeat the motion. When Lynch was killed a fortnight later, however, de Valera renewed his appeal.

'I am afraid,' he wrote to one member of the executive, 'we shall have to face the inevitable sooner or later, bow to force and resort to other methods.'

Although privately working for peace, de Valera still maintained a hardline public stand. Following Lynch's death, for example, he issued a statement eulogising the dead leader and referring to the Republican cause as an immortal one that would ultimately be successful. He made some peace overtures to the Cosgrave government — the most significant aspect of which was a demand that nobody should be excluded 'from the councils and parliament of the nation' for refusing to take an oath. Although his proposals were rejected, he nevertheless managed to persuade Frank Aiken, who had succeeded Lynch as Chief of Staff, to call off the campaign. Aiken simply ordered that the IRA should hide its arms and wait for more propitious circumstances in which to continue the struggle.

Following the cessation of hostilities, the Republicans reverted to a political approach, so de Valera again assumed the position of real leadership. He concentrated on criticising the Treaty — the overall implications of which were still far from clear. Because of the Civil War, for example, the Boundary Commission had not met, nor had the postponed financial issue been settled. He therefore contended that the people had 'not yet come to realise the humiliation of it all'.

'But,' he added, 'they soon will. The fate of the North-East Boundary clause and the amount of Ireland's share of the imperial burden will be determined sometime. When it is, and the Boundary clause has been waived, or some new ignominious bargain has been struck to evade it, and when, in addition, the full weight of an imperial contribution of some ten to fifteen millions annually is being pressed upon their shoulders, the people will surely wake up.' Then they would know the extent to which they had been misled and would appreciate 'what it is that those who gave their lives to prevent the consummation of this "Treaty" hoped to save them from'.

De Valera already had a plan to dismantle the Treaty. He outlined it privately in a letter on 21 June 1923. The one policy that ultimately had a chance of success was, he wrote:

(a) Maintaining that we are a sovereign state and ignoring as far as possible any conditions in the 'Treaty' that are inconsistent with that status – a policy of squeezing England out by a kind of boycott of the Gov. General etc.

(b) Breaching the 'Treaty' by the oath, smashing thro' that first and then compelling England to tolerate the breaches or bring her to a revision which would lead to something like the Doc. 2 position.

In order to implement that plan, however, it would first be necessary for the Republicans to regain power. In the interim he felt that the most desirable step was to 'manoeuvre into the position in which free speech' would be possible. If that could be done he was convinced that it would save years of effort and provide an opportunity in which 'we could give our opponents a real shaking'. But he was convinced that the govern- ment would 'do everything possible to prevent this'.

When Cosgrave called a general election in the summer of 1923, the Republicans decided to contest it under the Sinn Féin banner, and de Valera came out of hiding to address an election rally in Ennis. But he had just begun to speak when he was arrested by Free State troops. Even though he was easily re-elected, he was forced spend the next year in jail.

Upon being released de Valera continued to put increasing emphasis on the partition question. He defended the Stormont seat that he had won in South Down in 1921 and actually crossed the border to campaign in Newry, but he was arrested and served with an exclusion order by Northern Ireland authorities. Shortly afterwards he ignored that order and returned to the six counties for a speech in Derry, but he was again arrested and this time sentenced to a month in Belfast Jail.

When the Boundary Commission turned out to be a fiasco in 1925, the Free State government tried to make the best of a bad situation by waiving its claim to nationalist areas in return for some financial considerations, which certainly had the appearance of the 'ignominious bargain' that de Valera had predicted the previous year. Even though he had initially accepted the Boundary Commission scheme himself, he had long since begun to criticise that aspect of the Treaty and as the years passed the mistaken view became quite widespread that he had been opposed to the Treaty primarily on account of partition.

With the Cosgrave government apparently coming off worst in its relations with London, the time seemed right for de Valera to re-enter the Dáil. But he was faced with the problem of recognising the Free State. Prior to his arrest in 1923 he had been in favour of abstaining from the Dáil for basically tactical reasons, but while he was in jail Mary MacSwiney managed to perusade the party to take the more radical approach of refusing to recognise the Free State, its government, or its governmental institutions. And this policy had taken a firm hold by the time of his release, so that when he tried 'to bring the policy back to the point it should never have changed from', he ran into serious opposition from people who looked on his policy as 'a complete change of front'. Thus when he proposed that the Sinn Féin Ard Fheis should authorise its deputies to enter the Dáil, if that could be done without taking the oath, the proposal was narrowly defeated. De Valera therefore walked out and founded a new party, Fianna Fáil, of which he became the first leader.

In early 1927 he formally recognised the Free State by requesting a passport to travel to the United States, where he planned to raise money for the new party and also hoped to embarrass the Cosgrave government by blocking its efforts to get hold of more than two million dollars which he had deposited in the name of the Irish Republic while in America in 1920. He realised that he would not be able to get hold of the money himself, but he took the stand in order to prevent Free State authorities being recognised as the legitimate successors of the 1919–22 regime. Here de Valera had his first real political victory since his fall from power. The New York Supreme Court found that as the Irish Republic had never been officially recognised, the money should be returned to subscribers.

Bolstered with campaign funds collected by de Valera in the United States, Fianna Fáil fared spectacularly well in its first general election in June 1927 by winning forty-four seats — just two fewer than Cosgrave's ruling Cumann na nGaedheal. But when Fianna Fáil deputies tried to enter the Dáil, they were stopped and told that they would first have to subscribe their names to a book containing the oath. They refused and withdrew. Each of the deputies [75] then signed a statement to the effect that 'under no circumstances whatever' would they subscribe to that oath. De Valera's initial plan was to secure a constitutional amendment doing away with the oath by a plebiscite. At the time the Free State constitution stipulated that the signatures of only 75,000 eligible voters were necessary to call a referendum for a constitutional amendment. In view of Fianna Fáil's strength at the polls there was a good chance that this tactic would succeed, but the political climate was upset within a month by the assassination of Vice-President O'Higgins.

Even though the Fianna Fáil leader denounced the crime as murder, and totally dissociated his party from the killing, the Cosgrave government used the occasion to take steps to force Fianna Fáil deputies to swallow their pride on the question of the oath. A constitutional amendment was hurriedly passed doing away with referenda, and a further bill was introduced stipulating that deputies would forfeit their seats in the Dáil if these were not taken within two months.

Confronted with the legislation, de Valera felt that entering the Dáil was 'the *only* alternative to resigning ourselves to gradual extinction as an effective force'. He therefore decided to subscribe his name to the book containing the oath but made it clear beforehand that he was doing so as an empty gesture that was without 'binding significance in conscience or in law'.

'I am not prepared to take the oath', he told the clerk of the Dáil. 'I am not going to take it. I am prepared to put my name down here in this book in order to get permission to get into the Dáil, and it has no other significance.'

There was a Bible on the table, so de Valera picked it up and moved it to the other side of the room before returning to where the book lay. 'You must remember,' he again stressed, 'that I am not taking an oath.' He then signed his name.

Afterwards he said that he had signed the book in the same way that he would sign an autograph. 'If you whether I had any idea of what was there', he explained, 'I say, Yes, but it was not read to me, nor was I asked to read it.'

While de Valera undoubtedly satisfied his own conscience by categorically stating that he was only signing his name and not subscribing to the oath, there were those who felt that the whole affair would hurt Fianna Fáil's standing among the more radical segments of the population. De Valera himself thought that Cosgrave called another general election for that September — barely two months after the previous — in the belief that many Republicans would withdraw their support from Fianna Fáil over the oath. Although Cumann na nGaedheal gained twenty-one seats and were thus able to form a stable government with the help of one of the smaller parties, Fianna Fáil gained thirteen seats to firmly establish itself as the second-strongest party in the Dáil.

In the following years de Valera devoted much of his energies to strengthening Fianna Fáil at the local level — where the party built up a mass organisation based on a system of parish clubs, while Cumann na nGaedheal tended to rely on an elite in large town. De Valera also made a couple of fund-raising tours to the United States where he collected money to finance the launching of his own daily newspaper, the *Irish Press*. When it began publishing in September 1931, the country was in the throes of the Great Depression and there was no shortage of issues on which it could berate the government, which had not only been following austere financial policies with an almost masochistic zeal, but had also re-introduced military tribunals to deal with growing political violence.

With the government's mandate running out, Cosgrave called a general election for January 1932. He was obviously hoping to capitalise on the recent enactment of the Statute of Westminster, in accordance with which Britain had formally acknowledged that all of the dominions, including the Irish Free State, were sovereign in their own domestic affairs and were equal partners within the British Commonwealth. In effect, it made *de jure* what had been the *de facto* status of the dominions at the time of the Treaty negotiations. Cosgrave obviously hoped that Cumann na nGaedheal would be returned to power on the stregth of the clarification of the country's status, coupled with the exploitation of fears that many people had about de Valera.

For years various smear tactics had been used to depict him as a dangerous and malignant ogre by defaming his political, religious, and moral integrity. There was, for example, a whispering campaign about his relationship with a number of women, especially his secretary, Kathleen O'Connell. From 1916 to 1924 he had certainly had little family life, as he spent most of his time away from home, either in America, in jail, or in hiding. It was in the United States that he first met Kathleen O'Connell in 1919. She then returned to Ireland and went into hiding with him, which led to some malicious gossip about their relationship. These rumours were published in the American press, but no Irish newspaper dared print the gossip and thus risk a legal action under the country's more stringent libel laws. On one occasion de Valera appeared to lose his temper over the slanderous stories. He complained to a stunned Dáil about malicious rumours to the effect that his wife had left him and that he was supposedly having simultaneous affairs with two or three women. 'It is part of a campaign,' he said, 'and as long as people pander to that sort of thing you are not going to have any respect here for the so-called will of the people.'

[78] The smear tactics included suggestions that de Valera was a communist — a charge fraught with implications beyond that of subscribing to a radical social or political ideology. It raised the highly emotive spectre of militant atheism and reminded people that he and his Republican colleagues had, by their Civil War activities, disregarded the threat of excommunication from the Roman Catholic Church.

'I am not a communist', he had to declare during the 1932 election campaign. 'I am quite the reverse.' He emphasised that he wanted to create a greater number of individual property owners by distributing land and increasing the number of homesteads on it. He therefore contended that his opponents were simply manufacturing a red scare in order to bolster their own waning political fortunes.

In the course of the campaign de Valera concentrated on Fianna Fáil's election manifesto, which listed party goals like the revival of the Gaelic language, the ending of partition, the abolition of the oath, and the suspension of annuity payments to Britain that were being made without the formal approval of the Dáil. The manifesto also emphasised the need for alternative economic policies, such as the redistribution of land and the introduction of protective tariffs in order to foster native industries that would alleviate the chronic unemployment situation. Although primarily interested in political aims, like the removal of the oath, he had for long believed that alternative economic policies could be used to attract the necessary support to enable himself and his colleagues to fulfil their political goals. As early as 1924, for instance, he wrote that they should 'stand for fair play and justice between all classes, and push co-operation and such enterprises as will be of advantage to all. The more we lean to the economic side the better it will be for the political objective but it must be a national

programme for the common good not a class programme.'
By making an issue of the various annuity payments
that were being made to Britain, especially the land
annuities arising out of the land purchase legislation
passed around the turn of the century, de Valera
was able to exploit the anti-British sentiment that was
still rife in the country. He actually equated the
annuity payments with the war reparations imposed
on Germany following the Great War. At the time the
German payments were popularly believed to be so
heavy that they had undermined the world economy.
The Fianna Fáil leader noted, however, that the Free
State was being asked to pay comparatively more to
Britain annually, than Germany's total annual payments. And he added the emotive charge that the
Irish people were actually paying for damage that had
been done by the British during the War of Independence.

The Fianna Fáil appeal was obviously successful,
because the party gained enough seats to become the
largest party in the Dáil and, with the help of the
Labour Party, was able to form a government. De
Valera was therefore returned to power as President
of the Executive Council of the Irish Free State barely
ten years after his resignation as President of the Irish
Republic's Dáil.

6

Using the Stepping-Stones

De Valera put together a government that included
many strong-willed individuals. Yet he was able to in-
stil in it an extraordinary cohesiveness. Of course his
ministerial colleagues undoubtedly shared his general

outlook, seeing that they had sided with him in the
[80] split that led to the formation of Fianna Fáil. But
part of his secret undoubtedly lay in a combination
of his own tremendous patience and his magnetic
charm, which even some of his bitterest political
opponents freely acknowledged. For in spite of his
public image as a dour, austere individual, he was really
a charming person with a good sense of humour.

According to Seán Lemass, a member of that first
Fianna Fáil government, the new President's style of
leadership was to seek agreed decisions on overall
policy by relying 'upon the force of physical exhaustion to get agreement'. He would not allow consideration of any subject to end with a vote. Instead, he
sought 'unanimity by the simple process of keeping
the debate going – often till the small hours of the
morning, until those who were in the minority, out of
sheer exhaustion, conceded the case made by the
majority'. As he personally possessed an almost in-
exhaustible store of patience, it meant that he almost
always got his own way. Thus, to use the title of one
of his earlier biographies, he was a *Unique Dictator*.

De Valera retained the portfolio of External Affairs
himself, which meant that much of his time was
taken up with foreign policy matters, especially relations with Britain. From the outset his policy was
obviously to follow the course he had outlined in
1923 of 'squeezing England out' by boycotting the
Governor-General and 'breaching the "Treaty"' by
discarding the oath and 'then compelling England to
tolerate the breaches or bring her to a revision which
would lead to something like the Doc. 2 position'.

After taking office, members of the government
refused to attend functions to which the Governor-
General had been invited. While there was no formal
announcement of that policy, it quickly became
apparent when the *Irish Press* reported that Vice-
President Seán T. O'Kelly and Defence Minister

Frank Aiken had walked out of a social function at the French Legation upon the arrival of the Governor- General, James MacNeill. When the latter protested over the snub, de Valera expressed regret and promised that a similar occurence would not happen again if MacNeill informed him of his 'public social engagements' in advance. In other words, members of the government intended to boycott the Governor-General but would do so discreetly if he cooperated.

In April 1932 the government introduced legislation to abolish the oath. Although there was considerable doubt at the time about whether the Free State had the right to unilaterally alter the Treaty, de Valera contended that the Statute of Westminster, which guaranteed that the Free State and the other dominions could determine their own domestic policies, had provided the necessary authority. As a result of that statute he explained that the Free State had virtually secured the status he was seeking in 1921 when he proposed Document No. 2.

'The twenty-six counties', he told the Senate, 'had practically got into the position — with the sole exception that instead of being a republic it was a monarchy'. In that speech de Valera came as near to admitting publicly that he had been wrong in the whole Treaty controversy as he would ever come. 'I am prepared to confess,' he continued, 'that there have been advances made that I did not believe would be made at the time.'

Although the government's efforts to abolish the oath were frustrated by delaying tactics in the Senate, de Valera moved ahead and actually suggested that the British should accept a revision of the Treaty that would formally bring it into line with External Association. In June 1932 he candidly told two Britsh ministers who visited Dublin for talks that he was anxious for amicable relations with Britain. But he added that the only basis for lasting friendship would be if Ireland were recognised as a thirty-two county republic. Once that had been done, he said that the island would probably agree to being freely associated with Britain. However, the British were no more prepared to accept that in 1932 than they had been a decade earlier.

During the talks de Valera showed himself to be amenable to discussions with the British on financial matters. In fact, he seemed eager to negotiate, which was understandable seeing that he did have a fairly good case, especially on the land annuities question. The Partition Act of 1920 had specified that the annuities were to be handed over to the respective parliaments in Dublin and Belfast. But in 1923 Cosgrave had assumed that the Free State was obligated to pay the annuities and he signed a secret agreement to do so. De Valera was surprised when the British mentioned that agreement. He had never even heard of it, so a search was ordered for the document.

The Irish copy was in very poor condition when found. 'It is literally in tatters', the President told the Dáil, 'half-pages, parts of pages not typed, interlineations and so on. Honestly, I never saw a contract of any kind presented in such a form. There is not even an Irish signature to it.'

Cosgrave had signed the British copy, but de Valera was not prepared to accept it as binding because the Dáil had never ratified the agreement. In fact, the only kind of ratification to which the British could point was the rather extraordinary contention that the agreement had been popularly ratified by Cosgrave's return to power following the general election held some weeks later. Of course it was preposterous to contend that the Irish electorate had ratified an agreement, when they were ignorant of its very existence — not to mention its specifics.

But even if the 1923 agreement had obligated the Free State to pay the annuities, de Valera contended that the 1925 agreement doing away with the Boundary Commission had cancelled that obligation by [83] specifically releasing the Dublin government from its obligation to service the British public debt. At least one British authority privately admitted in March 1932 that the Irish had 'an arguable point'. Neville Chamberlain, then Chancellor of the Exchequer, noted that the wording of the Boundary Commission agreement absolved the Dublin government 'from liability for the service of the Public Debt of the United Kingdom, and the Irish annuities form part of the Public Debt'. Consequently he observed that there was 'a certain risk that an arbitrator might hold that Mr de Valera is right from a purely legal and technical point of view, and it would seem most undesirable that we should expose ourselves to such a decision'.

Even though de Valera was prepared to submit the question to the arbitration of a broad international tribunal, the British insisted on a Commonwealth tribunal. The whole question was becoming inextricably linked with the broader constitutional question of the Free State's membership of the British Commonwealth. The British were afraid that agreeing to an international tribunal with members from outside the Commonwealth would be tantamount to acknowledging a distinction between the Free State and the other dominions, so they insisted that the tribunal could be composed only of representatives from within the Commonwealth. But since all of the other dominions looked to Britain as their mother country, the President contended that such a commission would be biased in favour of Britain. Convinced that the Free State had been seriously wronged by the Boundary Commission – presided over by a South African judge – de Valera was not about to take the chance of being wronged again.

When the Fianna Fáil government withheld the

annuity payment due in July 1932, the British re-
[84] taliated by introducing a 20 per cent *ad valorem* tax
on Irish imports as an alternative means of collecting
the lost revenues. Dublin, in turn, imposed similar
levies on British imports. So began the Economic War
that was to last for almost six years.

As each country was the other's best customer, the
resulting economic dislocation was significant to
each, but the Irish were most seriously affected because Britain was virtually their only customer. In
fact, 96 per cent of all Irish exports went to Britain.
Nevertheless the Economic War was a kind of mixed
blessing from the Fianna Fáil standpoint. Cattle exports were most seriously affected, so farmers were
compelled to turn increasingly to tillage – one of the
party's more cherished goals. In addition, de Valera
was able to adopt protectionist policies in order to
foster Irish industries in the hope of building an
economy sufficiently strong and viable to stand independently of Britain. He travelled throughout the
country appealing to the strong nationalistic instincts
of the Irish people to support his government's
policies by buying Irish-made goods.

The difficulties over the annuities, however, were
not really the main problem as far as the British were
concerned. Sir Thomas Inskip, their Attorney-General,
publicly explained that there would be little difficulty
in resolving the difference between the two governments were it not for the constitutional implications
of de Valera's overall policy. 'If there could be a clear
and sincere declaration of the desired intention of
the Irish Free State to stay within the Empire on the
basis of their constitutional position and in a spirit of
loyal partnership,' Inskip declared, 'no annuities or
debts could cloud the prospect.'

The boycotting of the Governor-General had led to
a dispute which culminated in de Valera demanding
MacNeill's removal. At first the British asked for

details of the dispute, but the President refused to explain his motives. He simply insisted that his government was acting within its rights. London then somewhat reluctantly conceded the point.

After unsuccessfully trying to get the British to do away with the office, the government nominated a member of Fianna Fáil to fill it. He then took up residence in the Dublin suburbs, instead of at the Vice-Regal Lodge in Phoenix Park. The only official function that he performed was to affix his signature to acts of the legislature. De Valera had thereby successfully minimised the significance of the office and would, in fact, abolish it altogether little over three years later.

There was a brief glimmer of hope for an Anglo-Irish settlement in October 1932 when de Valera and three ministerial colleagues went to London for two days of formal talks, but it soon became apparent that each side considered its own position fundamental, so no progress was made. The President felt that British intransigence was being encouraged by Irish elements.

'I have come to the conclusion', he told the Dáil upon his return, 'that the British government, pressed forward as it is by certain anti-Irish feelings in Britain and supported by the attitude of a minority in this country, is not prepared to examine this position on its merits or to yield to claims of simple justice.' He implied that the Cosgrave opposition was implicated, and this has since been confirmed by British cabinet records.

Nevertheless there could be no doubt that the London government was encouraged in its intransigence by its own hope that the economic dislocation would undermine the Fianna Fáil government and lead to a return of Cosgrave's party, which would undoubtedly be more accommodating to the British. The opposition had unquestionably been adopting obstructionist tactics. Even though Michael Collins had advocated

accepting the Treaty as a mere stepping-stone to
[86] more complete freedom, some of his followers were
invoking his name in 1932 as if the agreement had
been intended as a permanent settlement. As a result
of their struggle against those who had tried to wreck
the Treaty a decade earlier, these people had apparently become inflexible in their support of the document.
'Those of us who supported the Treaty in 1922,
and those of us who fought to maintain it', one former Cumann na nGaedheal minister declared, 'will
consider ourselves traitors – to the memory of Collins
and O'Higgins and of the scores of National Army
men who gave their lives that the Treaty might be
secured for the people of this state – when we desert
the cause that they died for and go over to those who
were responsible for their deaths.'[31] The bitterness
engendered by the Civil War was still so intense that
many Cumann na nGaedheal people were opposing
policies which had had the active support of their
party in the past, simply because de Valera and
Fianna Fáil now espoused them.
In such a climate there was growing political unrest
throughout the country. The Fianna Fáil government
had dissolved the military tribunals and freed those
convicted under them, with the result that radical
Republican elements became more vocal, and Cumann
na nGaedheal meetings were frequently disrupted by
thugs declaring that there should be 'no free speech
for traitors'. Cumann na nGaedheal people reacted by
turning for protection to a quasi-military organisation
of their own, the Army Comrades Association (ACA).
By late 1932 there were distinct signs that the
opposition was coalescing. For example, James Dillon,
who as an independent member of the Dáil had
actually supported de Valera's election as President
earlier in the year, helped to found the National
Centre Party, which was gaining significant support

among the farming community, where there was considerable discontent both on account of the disas- trous drop in cattle exports and a misunderstanding over the land annuities question. Many farmers had thought that de Valera had been promising to abolish the annuities, whereas he had only proposed to withhold them from the British. He still intended that the Land Commission should collect the payments for the Irish exchequer.

The National Centre Party entered negotiations with Cumann na nGaedheal in the hope of uniting politically. But before they could combine de Valera called a surprise general election.

The ensuing campaign was probably the bitterest in the state's history. The opposition ran a more positive campaign, but it seemed to be simply trying to outflank Fianna Fáil by adopting modifications of the President's own policies. For instance, Cosgrave promised that if he got back into power, he would cancel the arrears of land annuities, declare a moratorium on their payment for 1934, and would negotiate to have them reduced thereafter. He also promised to end the Economic War, arrange a trade agreement with Britain, and secure a revision of the previous financial settlement by 'courageous negotiations'. Those promises prompted de Valera's supporters to declare in their election advertisements that 'Even Cosgrave admits that Fianna Fáil was right all the time'.

Fianna Fáil duly increased its Dáil representation and won an outright majority of its own. Though it was the slimmest majority possible – 77 out of 153 seats, the party could still rely on the support of the Labour Party, which had increased its representation to eight seats. De Valera was therefore easily re-elected as President.

One of the first acts of the new government was to remove the Commissioner of the Garda Siochana,

General Eoin O'Duffy, who had unquestionably been [88] acting in a biased political manner. Even though he had been offered another position within the Civil Service, his removal as Commissioner was seen by many people as an indication that Fianna Fáil was going back on its promise not to victimise people who had served Cumann na nGaedheal governments. O'Duffy therefore became a kind of martyr in opposition circles. And when Cumann na nGaedheal and the National Centre Party merged to form the United Ireland Party (or Fine Gael as it later became more commonly known), he was elected its first leader. He also became leader of the ACA, which began modelling itself on fascist lines under his guidance. Copying the Blackshirts in Italy and the Brownshirts in Nazi Germany, each member of the ACA adopted a blue shirt as his uniform, and the organisation became known as the Blueshirts. They found considerable support among pro-Treaty elements, who understandably felt that they needed such an organisation to protect them from the IRA, which had been harassing them while the government seemed at best indifferent to their plight. The Blueshirts became so strong under O'Duffy's somewhat irrational leadership that there were genuine fears for a time that they might attempt a fascist-style *coup d'état*. The government therefore outlawed the wearing of such uniforms and proscribed private armies.

In order to enforce these laws the military tribunals, which de Valera had criticised so vociferously while in opposition, were again re-introduced. At first these were only used against the Blueshirts, but it was not long before the government also found itself compelled to use them against members of the IRA, who were responsible for a number of murders during the mid 1930s. The most notable of the killings occurred in March 1936 when Boyle Somerville, a seventy-year-old retired Royal Navy admiral, was murdered because he had obliged some local men who had sought his help in joining the British navy.

De Valera denounced the crime and had the IRA outlawed. 'If one section of the community could claim the right to build up a political army,' he explained, 'so could another, and it would not be long before this country would be rent asunder by rival military factions.' He added that 'if a minority tries to have its way by force against the will of the majority it is inevitable that the majority will resist by force, and this can only mean civil war.'

Opponents were quick to note that de Valera was talking in terms that differed greatly from 1922 when he had maintained that the minority had a right to uphold its views with arms. Even though Cosgrave, who had replaced O'Duffy as leader of the United Ireland Party, agreed with the suppression of the IRA, he cynically observed that the President was a recent convert to democracy.

Whether de Valera saw the incongruity in his own words may be open to question, but there can be little doubt that he believed that he had played an honourable role in the events leading to the Civil War. He thought that the Collins faction had been primarily responsible for that conflict. Indeed he was so convinced of this that he challenged Cosgrave to agree to the setting up of a historical commission to look into the whole matter.

The President proposed that Cosgrave and himself should each nominate three people such as a judge, a constitutional lawyer, a professor, or a recognised student of history to serve on the commission and to ask the Roman Catholic hierarchy to nominate a bishop to act as an impartial chairman. Each side would then make all of its documents available to the commission. Cosgrave's blunt rejection of the challenge could only have further strengthened de Valera's conviction in the propriety of his own actions of 1922.

Ever since the Civil War, relations between de Valera and Cosgrave had been embittered. Except on the floor of the Dáil, they did not speak to one another, and they would carry that feud almost to the end of their lives. In view of what had happened in 1922 their mutual distrust was understandable, but de Valera's feelings were certainly not helped by the whispering campaign that some people in Cosgrave's party were still carrying on against him. There was snide insinuations, for example, about his foreign background, his religious heritage, and even his legitmacy. One 'dirty innuendo' that particularly irritated him – for which he blamed the opposition – was a suggestion that he was the bastard son of a Spanish Jew.

'There is not, so far as I know, a single drop of Jewish blood in my veins', de Valera declared in obvious frustration in the Dáil. 'On both sides I come from Catholic stock. My father and mother were married in a Catholic church on September 19th 1881. I was born in October 1882. I was baptised in a Catholic church. I was brought up here in a Catholic home.' He added that he did not care who tried to pretend that he was not Irish. 'I say I have been known to the Irish and that I have given everything in me to the Irish nation.'

Over the years de Valera protested his Irishness so much that he seemed to betray an insecurity about his foreign background. According to his authorised biographers, he was actually known as Edward Coll during his younger years, which possibly indicated a certain sensitivity about his Spanish surname. As children can be very cruel, it was not unlikely that during those formative years playmates and fellow-pupils teased him about his background to the extent that he developed an unconscious insecurity about merely being a 'blow-in', to use the memorable words of one of his successors. If he did suffer from that

kind of subconscious insecurity, it was indeed ironic
that he should eventually become the virtual personification of Ireland in the eyes of many people. He
owed that reputation largely to his accomplishments
in the area of external affairs, in which he relentlessly
persisted in his efforts to demonstrate Irish independence by dismantling the 1921 Treaty.

Following the general election of 1933, the President publicly declared that his policy was to remove
unilaterally the disagreeable aspects of the Treaty.
Speaking at Arbour Hill that April he said that he was
not prepared willingly to 'assent to any form of
symbol' that was inconsistent with the country's
status as a sovereign nation. 'Let us remove these
forms one by one', he declared, 'so that this State
that we control may be a Republic in fact; and that,
when the time comes, the proclaiming of the Republic may involve no more than a ceremony, the formal
confirmation of a status already attained.'

Within a month he had finally achieved the formal
abolition of the oath, which had been delayed by the
Senate the previous year. Then in August the government introduced legislation limiting the country's
connection with the British Crown by curtailing the
powers of the Governor-General and by abolishing
the right of appeal to the judicial committee of the
Privy Council. The following year three further
bills were introduced giving effect to de Valera's
concept of reciprocal citizenship first advocated in
1921.

By the time the bills became law, confusion about
the legality of the unilateral dismantling of the Treaty
had been eliminated by a finding of the judicial committee of the British Privy Council, which ruled that
while Dublin had no authority to abrogate the treaty
prior to 1931, the Statute of Westminster had thereafter conferred the necessary powers of abrogation.

Following that decision the British softened somewhat their hardline approach to Irish affairs. They [92] indicated that Dublin had the right to eliminate even the remaining connections with the Crown, but they warned that this would mean leaving the British Commonwealth with the consequent denial of the privileges of British citizenship to Irish people living in the dominions. It was hoped that the realisation that the adoption of Republican symbols would necessitate withdrawal from the Commonwealth might persuade de Valera not to include any objectionable items in a new constitution that he was planning to propose.

When a constitutional crisis arose in Britain over the abdication of King Edward VIII, however, de Valera seized on the occasion to take a far-reaching step towards formal External Association. He had earlier advised that the King should be allowed to marry a divorcee seeing that divorce was legal in Britain, but when the crisis was brought to a head and the dominions were asked to legitimise the abdication, the Dublin government used the occasion to clarify the real position of the British King in Irish affairs. The President explained that he wanted that position to be clearly understood from the very moment of the new King's accession to the throne.

The External Relations Act, by which the Irish legislation was known, stipulated that as long as the Free State was associated with the various dominions and while they continued to recognise the British King 'as the symbol of their co-operation' in such matters as the appointment of diplomatic and consular representatives, then the Executive Council had the authority to advise the King to act on behalf of the Irish Free State in such matters. The wording of that legislation emphasised, however, that the King would only act on the advice of the Executive Council, which would be free to decide whether or not to actually ask the monarch to act on behalf of the Irish people.

Britain was suddenly confronted with a *fait accompli*. The cabinet's committee on Irish affairs held an urgent meeting to consider whether the External Relations Act provided the minimum 'necessary to secure membership of the British Commonwealth'. By all previous reckonings, the legislation clearly did not, but the British were obviously anxious not to complicate the abdication crisis. They decided that the Irish actions did not alter the country's standing within the Commonwealth seeing that Article I of the existing Free State constitution, which declared the country to be 'a co-equal member of the Community of Nations forming the British Commonwealth of Nations', had not been tampered with.

But much to the dismay of the British, de Valera dropped that article from the new constitution that he introduced some months later. It was a purely Republican document. There was no mention of any ties with the British Crown or Commonwealth and the new head of state was to be a popularly elected President. All mention of any connection with Britain was left to ordinary legislation. The External Relations Act remained on the statute books, but unlike the provisions of the constitution, which were ratified by popular referendum on 1 July 1937 and could therefore be amended only by the Irish electorate, the terms of the External Relations Act could be changed at will by the Irish legislature.

In less than five years de Valera, who relinquished the title of President of the Executive Council to become Taoiseach (chief) under the new constitution, had dismantled the most disagreeable aspects of the 1921 Treaty. With the sole exception of the Ulster question, he had proved that Collins had been right in contending that the Treaty provided the freedom to achieve freedom. And even on the Ulster issue de Valera had achieved what he had himself advocated should be done during the Treaty debate. For instance,

Article 2 of the new constitution claimed sovereignty [94] over the whole thirty-two counties of Ireland, but the following article stipulated that 'pending the reintegration of the national territory', the laws enacted in Dublin would extend only to the twenty-six counties. In other words, Northern Ireland's existence was accepted, but its right to exist was not formally recognised, just as he had advocated should be done back in December 1921.

As it was hoped that the constitution would ultimately apply to the whole island, de Valera wanted to ensure that it would not need any basic change once unity had been effected so, subject to 'public order and morality,' there were guarantees of 'fundamental rights' such as freedom of speech, conscience, association, and assembly, *habeas corpus,* and inviolability of one's home. In addition, all citizens were recognised as equal before the law and there was protection against religious discrimination, but the constitution nevertheless accorded closely with Roman Catholic thinking. 'The Most Holy Trinity' was attributed as the source of all authority, and the Roman Catholic Church was recognised as having a 'special position' in the state 'as the guardian of the Faith professed by the great majority of citizens'. Divorce was prohibited in order to protect the family, which was described 'as the natural primary and fundamental unit group of society, and as a moral institution possessing inalienable and imprescriptible rights, antecedent and superior to all positive law.' There was also a further stipulation that the state should try to ensure that mothers would 'not be obliged by economic necessity to engage in labour to the neglect of their duties in the home'.

The constitution actually incorporated an outline of liberal social principles 'for the general guidance' of the legislature. Those guiding ideals envisioned the state attempting to ensure that all citizens would have an adequate means of livelihood, that they would be protected against exploitation by private industry, and that the material resources of the nation would be distributed in such a way as best to serve 'the common good.' In particular, it was advocated that as many families as practicable should 'be established on the land in economic security'. The state was also urged to safeguard 'the economic interests of the weaker sections of the community' and to ensure that the health of workers should 'not be abused,' and that they should 'not be forced by economic necessity to enter avocations unsuited to their sex, age or strength.'

Since those principles were simply for the general guidance of the legislature and were specifically placed outside the jurisdiction of the courts, some people viewed them as mere platitudes, but it was not inappropriate that they should be mentioned boldly in the constitution, if only as a constant reminder that parliamentarians should strive to attain those lofty ideals. Moreover, from the strictly political standpoint, de Valera and his colleagues undoubtedly had their standing enhanced by the impression that they were striving for the implementation of the social principles outlined.

The constitutional emphasis on family life also probably helped to boost de Valera's image as a dedicated family man. However his family life in fact had had to take second place to de Valera's political concerns for a considerable period.

Prior to becoming involved in the Easter Rebellion, for example, he had made no provisions for his pregnant wife and four children, with the result that they were left virtually destitute. His wife had to move in with her parents and the older children were scattered among relatives. After his release from jail the following year, the family was reunited, but de Valera himself quickly left to campaign for the East Clare by-election, and then following his victory, spent much of his time touring the country before again being imprisoned for his supposed part in the so-called German Plot. He actually spent most of the next six years in jail, in America, or on the run. Even after his release from internment following the Civil War he spent two prison stints in Belfast and made three extended visits to the United States. As a result some of his children hardly knew him.

'My first recollection of a normal situation', his youngest son, Terry, wrote, 'was to have my father in America and my mother at home'. He added that his father 'meant little more than the tall, dark-haired, bespectacled, severe figure who occasionally appeared on the home scene'. After Fianna Fáil came to power in 1932 his father began spending more time at home and it was only then that eleven-year-old Terry first got to know him. By that time the older children were in their late teens and early twenties.

'As a child', Terry's older brother, Eamonn, recalled, 'I feared my father, and resented his intrusion into our lives.' The oldest of the girls, Mairin, recalled a story about two of her younger brothers, Ruari and Brian. 'Who is Dev?' one of them asked one day. 'I think he's Mummy's father', was the other's pathetic reply. When the fifth child, Brian, died after a riding accident in 1936, there was only one photograph of the whole family together. As a result there can be little doubt that de Valera's dedication to the nationalist cause was such that his family life had suffered.

Although he could have felt satisfied that the new constitution had gone a long way towards the realisation of Irish national aspirations by further dismantling the 1921 Treaty, the majority of the Irish electorate were obviously not satisfied with the government's performance. Following a general election held on the same day as the referendum on the constitution, Fianna Fáil lost its overall majority in the Dáil

and again became dependent on the support of the
Labour Party. Over the years Fianna Fáil had antago-
nised some of its previous support, especially in
republican quarters. Other were disillusioned with the
nationalism that pervaded not only political, but also
economic and cultural life in the twenty-six counties.
According to one of his more sympathetic biographers, Mary Bromage, de Valera espoused a 'puri-
tanical morality'. It was popularly believed that he
disapproved of smoking and drinking, but that was
not all. 'His strictures,' Bromage wrote, 'extended
beyond the evils of drink to the evils of jazz, the evils
of betting on the races, the dangers from indecent
books, and he concurred in the Government's bill to
censor publications. The literary censorship, he
urged, should be aimed at sexual immorality and
should apply not only to books and moving-pictures
but to the Sunday papers as well because they reached
so many people.' Virtually every Irish writer of international distinction had a book banned by the censorship board during the 1930s, with the result that
some of the most articulate critics of de Valera's
government were to be found in the literary world.
But these people probably influenced few outside
their own circles. It was more likely that the decline
in Fianna Fáil support was attributable to factors
resulting from the continuing Economic War.
    The British had started the economic confronta-
tion with their punitive tarriffs following Dublin's
withholding of the land annuities, but, as was mentioned earlier, de Valera welcomed the opportunity
that the whole affair afforded his government to
appeal to the nationalistic instincts of the Irish people
to remodel their economic system so that it would be
strong enough to stand independently of Britain. He
told the Senate that the country had an opportunity
to build 'the foundation here of the sort of economic
life that every Irishman who thought nationally in

the past has hoped for'. An intensive campaign to make the country self-sufficient was launched, with industrial expansion being encouraged, as efforts were made to promote Irish goods at home and find new markets for them abroad.

The resulting economic dislocation was somewhat traumatic and de Valera had to endure opposition gibes that his policy of self-sufficiency would, in effect, leave the Irish people without a shirt on their backs. But he was unapologetic. 'That is the policy that is going to reduce us to the hair shirt and *bainín,*' he exclaimed defiantly in the Dáil. 'If we did come in here in *bainíní*, we would not be a bit colder than we are and we might look just as well.'

Public discontent was undoubtedly tempered by the realisation that a share of the economic hardships was also being borne by members of the government who had, after all, drastically cut their own salaries upon coming to power. Moreover, even though the economic picture was indeed gloomy, the government's programme did meet with some mixed results. There were, for instance, dramatic reductions in the importation of shoes, clothing, and bacon as native industries began to make an impact. Britain was actually hurt when her share of the Irish import market declined from the 81 per cent of 1931 to 50 per cent in 1937, but Irish efforts to find new international markets were a dismal failure: only 5 per cent of the country's exports were redirected, which meant that a staggering 91 per cent still went to Britain. At the same time the value of Irish exports to Britain dropped by 50 per cent, which led to a record trade deficit of £20.7 millions in 1937. In addition, Irish authorities were really paying the annuities indirectly by providing export subsidies to mitigate the effects of the British import duties. Consequently in late 1937 de Valera formally proposed that the British should agree to negotiate a settlement of Anglo-Irish differences.

7

The Great Statesman

In settling Irish difficulties with Britain de Valera was helped by the enviable reputation he had carved out for himself as a statesman at the League of Nations over the years. Upon coming to power in 1932 his government inherited a seat on the Council of the League and he made effective use of it to redeem himself in the eyes of the international community. It so happened that when the League met in September 1932, it was the Free State's turn to take the presidency of the Council, which revolved every three months. De Valera therefore took the chair and acquitted himself with distinction.

As President of the Council, he made the opening address to the Assembly. It was obvious that his reputation as an enemy of the League — resulting from his campaign against American ratification of the Versailles Treaty — had preceded him. When he rose to speak there was none of the customary politeness normally shown to a speaker. He was greeted with an eerie silence.

De Valera's address, which he wrote himself, was one of remarkable simplicity and common sense. It spotlighted the League's shortcomings and emphasised the need to strengthen the organisation in order to provide it with the influence necessary to achieve its worthy aims. In an obvious reference to the recent Japanese invasion of Manchuria, he stressed that 'no state should be permitted to jeopardise the common interest by selfish action, contrary to the Covenant.' The one way of enlisting the support of millions of apathetic people was to demonstrate that the Covenant was 'a solemn pact, the obligations of which no state, great or small, will find it possible to ignore.'

On finishing the address, de Valera sat down to 'a

stony silence unbroken by a single note of applause'.
[100] He had obviously dumbfounded his listeners. It was
not that they disagreed with what he had said. Even
British correspondents who had for long been critical
of the Irish leader reported that most delegates were
afterwards complimentary towards the address, as
were the various international newsmen. 'Mr de Valera
this morning made the best speech I ever heard from
a President of the League', the correspondent of the
London *Daily Herald* reported. 'That is not only my
own judgment. It is the opinion of almost every
League journalist with whom I have spoken.' According
to the *New York Times,* the Irish leader was unquestionably 'the outstanding personality' of the
session.

In the following weeks de Valera energetically
supported moves to secure the withdrawal of Japanese
forces from Manchuria. The Free State actually co-
sponsored a resolution in the Assembly calling on the
League to take action 'with a view to ensuring a
settlement of the dispute on the basis' of a commis-
sioned investigation which was very critical of Japan.
The Irish efforts went for naught, however, in the
face of the timidity of the major powers, especially
Britain and France, who temporised for fear of
offending the Japanese.

When other thorny questions arose later de Valera
again took strong stands in favour of the League, even
when his actions might have been expected to be
unpopular at home with the Irish people. For instance,
he supported the entry of the Soviet Union into the
international organisation even though it exposed him
to renewed charges of being a communist. But his
most vocal stands were in the cause of international
peace. During the Chaco War between Bolivia and
Paraguay, for example, he actually made what the
New York Times described as the 'sensational suggestion' that the League should establish a peace-keeping

force to keep the belligerents apart. He took an equally strong stand during the Ethiopian crisis of 1935.

'The final test of the League and all that it stands for has come,' de Valera told the League Assembly on 16 September 1935. 'Our conduct in this crisis will determine whether it is better to let it lapse and disappear and be forgotten.' He left no doubt that he believed that if the Italian dictator, Benito Mussolini, were allowed to go ahead with his threatened invasion of Ethiopia, it would fatally damage the League as an effective organisation for peace.

'Make no mistake,' he explained, 'if on any pretext whatever we were to permit the sovereignty of even the weakest state amongst us to be unjustly taken away, the whole foundation of the League would crumble into dust.' He added that, 'Without universality, the League can only be a snare. If the Covenant is not observed as a whole for all and by all, then there is no Covenant.'

When the Italians ignored the international outcry and invaded Ethiopia a fortnight later, de Valera went on radio to explain the situation to the Irish people. He noted that Japan's violation of the Covenant had shaken the League to its very foundations a few years earlier. 'It is obvious,' he said, 'that if a second similar successful violation takes place, the League of Nations must disappear as an effective safeguard for individual members.' He stressed that he had 'consistently held that the obligations of the Covenant should be enforced. That was our position in the case of the Sino-Japanese conflict. That is our position in the present case.'

De Valera's unequivocal support of the League met with a certain amount of criticism at home as members of the opposition were critical that he had not tried to extract economic concessions from the British in return for supporting the British call for sanctions against Italy. Some people expressed cynical amusement that he was pursuing the same policy as the [102] British, but that cynicism drew an effective rejoinder from de Valera himself, who observed that a person on the road to Heaven would not turn around and go to Hell simply because his worst enemy was taking the same road. Likewise, he emphasised that he was determined to follow the correct path — regardless of whom he had to share it with.

But the British and French were really bent on appeasing the Italian dictator, with the result that the economic sanctions directed against Italy were only half-hearted measures. It soon became obvious that the sanctions were doomed to fail. With their failure went the Irish leader's faith in the League as a means of collective security. Henceforth he was determined to pursue a policy of neutrality and he made no secret of that determination.

'Despite our judicial equality here, in matters such as European peace the small states are powerless', he told the League Assembly on 2 July 1936. 'Peace is dependent upon the will of the great states. All the small states can do, if the statesmen of the greater states fail in their duty, is resolutely to determine that they will not become the tools of any great power, and that they will resist with whatever strength that they may possess every attempt to force them into a war against their will.'

Believing that another major war was virtually inevitable following the Ethiopian debacle, de Valera made it clear that his government was determined to remain neutral, with the result that he no longer considered the obligations of the League's Covenant as binding. In demonstrating his determination to pursue that policy he soon revealed that he was prepared to take courageous stands without regard to their popularity either in Geneva or at home in Ireland. During the Spanish Civil War, for example, he disregarded strong Irish sympathy for the Nationalist forces of General Franco and supported the policy of non-intervention adopted by most members of the League of Nations. Nevertheless he refused to support those non-interventionist states in September 1937 when they introduced a resolution advocating that the policy of non-intervention be abandoned, if all countries did not comply with it. While de Valera personally sympathised with the efforts to isolate the conflict, he was afraid that Germany and Italy would ignore the resolution and continue their active support of Franco, which might then provoke some of the non-interventionists to support the other side and thus lead 'to a fatal competition which could only result in a general European disaster.' He therefore abstained from voting on the resolution in order to demonstrate 'beyond any possibility of misunderstanding' that the Free State would not be committed to any course of action that 'might result from the termination of the non-intervention agreement.'

De Valera realised, however, that no matter how determined he might be to remain neutral, such a policy would not be realistically possible in any war involving Britain, if the British government exercised its rights to Irish facilities. As it was Britain already had control of three ports in the twenty-six counties, in accordance with the terms of the 1921 Treaty, which also gave her the right to any other facilities she might requrie 'in time of war or of strained relations with a foreign power'. Obviously no enemy of Britain would recognise Irish neutrality under such circumstances.

The whole issue of British bases in Ireland really posed a serious dilemma for the Dublin government. If de Valera denied Britain her Treaty rights to further bases, it could lead to problems with the British but, on the other hand, if he acceded to such a request, it would almost certainly lead to difficulties with the

IRA. It was therefore little wonder that he was [104] anxious to settle the ports issue before the outbreak of hostilities in Europe.

Explaining that his government was worried about the danger of a major European war, de Valera proposed that formal Anglo-Irish negotiations be held with a view to settling outstanding difficulties between the two countries. The British agreed, so arrangements were made for an Irish delegation consisting of de Valera and three ministerial colleagues to visit London for talks, which began on 17 January 1938 and culminated in formal agreement fourteen weeks later.

The British were, of course, well aware of de Valera's attitude on the various issues even before the talks began. He had been having informal discussions with the Dominions Secretary, Malcolm MacDonald, for the past two years. During those talks he had indicated that he wanted the British to renounce their rights to Irish bases and drop their claim to the land annuities, but he was primarily concerned with the partition question. In all their coversations, MacDonald wrote, the Irish leader had 'been at pains to emphasise' that 'no final settlement' between the two countries would be possible while partition lasted.

If all the outstanding difficulties could be settled, de Valera predicted that the Irish people would be likely to come to Britain's aid in a major war. But he said that there could be no formal assurance in the matter — the country would have to be free to decide what course to take when the time came. The one commitment that he was prepared to make was that Ireland would not allow herself to be used as a base for an attack on Britain. The Irish leader's sincerity was not doubted. 'I am convinced', MacDonald wrote, 'that he is really genuine in desiring whole-hearted friendship and co-operation between the Irish Free State and Great Britain.'

During the opening session of the London talks the British Prime Minister, Neville Chamberlain, gave strong indications that Britain would hand over the three ports, renounce her right to other facilities, drop her claim to the land annuities, and abandon her duties on Irish imports, but he emphasised that there could be no settlement of partition against the will of the majority in Northern Ireland. Privately he admitted that partition was an anachronism about which he could do nothing, because the British public would not stand for putting pressure on Belfast in the matter. The only real concessions that the British were demanding were that the Dublin government should remove its import duties on goods from Northern Ireland and that it should agree to pay some of the more than £25 millions that Britain claimed in outstanding debts that were exclusive of the land annuities.

De Valera initially argued that he could make no concessions unless partition were ended. He contended, for example, that by handing over the ports, Britain would only be returning what rightfully belonged to the Irish people, so she should not expect any concession. But once the British indicated their willingness to turn over the bases, he went a step further and actually looked for financial concessions for being prepared to take the facilities off their hands. To the utter amazement of the British leader, de Valera suggested that the Irish people might not welcome the ports, because they would have to undertake the financial burden of defending them.

'I am lost in admiration of Mr de Valera's skill in dialectics,' the astounded Chamberlain told his cabinet. It might have been better, he added sarcastically, 'to spare Mr de Valera the embarrassment of having the ports offered to him.'

Throughout the negotiations de Valera emphasised the need to end partition. If the British would use their influence to bring about a settlement, he convinced them that Dublin would allow them to use any facilities they might need in wartime, but they stressed that their hands were tied on the Ulster question. Chamberlain suggested that removing the duties on imports from the six counties might help to alleviate the Northern opposition to Irish unity, but the Taoiseach rejected the suggestion. The talks might actually have collapsed on that issue had it not been for the intervention of President Franklin D. Roosevelt of the United States.

The American President had been asked to intervene by de Valera, who explained that a complete reconciliation between the British and Irish would 'affect every country where the two races dwell together, knitting their national strength and presenting to the world a great block of democratic peoples interested in the preservation of peace.' He therefore asked Roosevelt to use his 'influence to get the British Government to realise what would be gained by reconciliation and to get them to move whilst there is time.'

Although Roosevelt refused to intervene formally, he did instruct Joseph P. Kennedy, the recently appointed Ambassador to Britain, to tell Chamberlain privately that the White House was anxious for an Irish settlement. When Kennedy delivered that message in mid March the talks were deadlocked over de Valera's refusal to phase out duties on imports from Northern Ireland. Roosevelt's intervention apparently provided the impetus for Chamberlain to drop his demand and formally conclude agreements renouncing Britain's rights to Irish bases and ending the Economic War by settling Britain's financial claims of more than £100 millions for a lump-sum payment of £10 millions. In addition Britain agreed to remove her duties on Irish imports, while the Dublin government was only obliged to review its own import duties and to pro-

vide preferential treatment to some British imports.
There was no doubt that de Valera got the better of the negotiations, as the only significant concession he made was to agree to pay £10 millions in settlement of British claims for more than ten times that amount. Nevertheless he skillfully played down his overall achievement.

'I have repeatedly stated my belief', he told the Dáil, 'that if we were making agreements on the basis of justice – if sheer equity was to decide these matters – instead of paying money to Britain, whether a big or a small sum, the payments should be made the other way.' He added that deputies could, if they wished, regard the £10 millions 'as ransom money' for the ports.

While de Valera was disappointed with his failure to secure Irish unity, he obviously realised that the Irish people looked very favourably on the agreements. He therefore capitalised on the situation by calling a general election in May 1938 after losing a minor vote in the Dáil. Although he adopted a statesmanlike posture during the campaign, his Tánaiste (Deputy Prime Minister), Seán T. O'Kelly, used a rather demagogic approach to make capital out of the recent negotiations. 'In the past six years look how we whipped John Bull every time,' he said at one election rally in Dublin. 'Look at the last agreement we made with her. We won all round us, we whipped her right, left and centre, and, with God's help, we shall do the same again.'

Fianna Fáil had a resounding victory at the polls by winning 52 per cent of the first-preference votes and securing an overall majority of fifteen seats, which was the largest that the party was ever to enjoy in the Dáil during de Valera's lifetime.

In the following months the Taoiseach demonstrated a distinct softening in his attitude towards Britain. He still maintained his determination to keep out of war, but he publicly talked about the possibility of enlisting British help, if Ireland were invaded by some continental power. He suggested, for instance, that if such an attack became likely, his government might even be prepared to engage in consultations with the British in advance. As the occupation of Ireland would be a danger to them, he observed that they would 'be interested in giving to us any aid that we might ask'. He did not completely rule out the possibility that Britain would invade, but in view of recent developments he did say that it was 'not likely to happen'. There was evidence in September 1938 that the *rapprochement* between him and the British was mutual, when the British delegation supported his successful candidacy for the Presidency of the Assembly of the League of Nations.

That September was, in de Valera's own words, 'a time of unparalleled anxiety'. Adolf Hitler, the German leader, was threatening to seize the Sudetenland and this seemed likely to lead to a war in which Britain and France would come to the aid of Czechoslovakia. When Chamberlain decided to go to Munich for talks on the issue, de Valera was asked to mobilise opinion within the League of Nations for a settlement.

Having been outspoken in favour of the League taking strong stands during the Manchurian, Chaco and Ethiopian crises, the Irish leader had by then become a proponent of appeasement. He had, for example, been unwilling to support the motion even implying that further steps might be taken if foreign troops were not withdrawn from Spain during the civil war there. Moreover, in December 1937, he had announced that his government was, in effect, officially recognising Italy's annexation of Ethiopia by appointing an Irish Minister to the Court of Victor Emmanuel III in his capacity as King of Italy and Emperor of Ethiopia. Such recognition violated the Covenant, which obligated members of the League to refrain from recognising the forceful annexation of territory.

It should therefore have been of little surprise that de Valera vociferously supported a policy of appeasing Hitler at Munich nine months later. But then the Irish leader believed that the Fuhrer had a just complaint — seeing that the Versailles Treaty had cut off Germans in the Sudetenland from Germany in disregard for the principle of self-determination. In fact, the Taoiseach saw a distinct parallel between the Sudeten problem and the situation in Northern Ireland. On his way to Geneva he told one prominent British politician that the Dublin government had its 'own Sudetens in Northern Ireland' and he sometimes considered 'the possibility of going over the boundary and pegging out the territory, just as Hitler was doing'.[32]

In his capacity as President of the Assembly, de Valera appealed for support for a settlement from the League and also from the United States, to which he made a special broadcast. The essence of his attitude was that Germany's just demands should be conceded. That might not prevent Hitler from going to war in an effort to obtain more than Germany was entitled to, but in that case he said that the Nazis would be exposed as aggressors and the possibility of fighting such a war could be faced 'with relative equanimity'.

'Despite certain preaching', de Valera declared, 'mankind *has* advanced, and the public conscience, in a clear case of aggression, will count, and may well be in a European war a decisive factor'. It was not that he thought that peace-loving people should always surrender to someone who would not be deterred by the horrors of war, but that they should 'concede unhesitatingly the demands of justice' and then adopt a policy of wait and see. 'To allow fears for the future to intervene and make us halt in rendering justice in the present, is not to be wise but to be foolish.'

Early on 30 September 1938 the ill-fated Munich

agreement was signed, so it was to a much relieved
[110] Assembly that de Valera delivered the closing address
later that day. Even though the League had played no
part in the Munich talks, he made another of his
many appeals for the organisation to take heart and
tackle the major unresolved questions that were leading to repeated crises. In that way he felt that 'the
confidence which, twenty years ago, was reposed in
the League may be justified and fulfilled.' In particular he thought that an attempt should be made to
settle the problems of national minorities. 'We have
seen the danger we run by leaving these problems un-
solved', he said.

In speaking about that issue de Valera was undoubtedly mindful of the situation in Northern Ireland. On his way back to Dublin, he called on Chamberlain in London and tried unsuccessfully to get him
to solve the partition question on the lines of the
Sudeten settlement.

Back in Dublin the Taoiseach publicly held out the
possibility of concluding an alliance with Britain in
return for the ending of partition. During a widely
publicised interview with a correspondent of the
London *Evening Standard* he explained that it was
'possible to visualise a critical situation arising in the
future in which a united free Ireland would be willing
to co-operate with Britain to resist a common attack.'
But he warned that 'no Irish leader will ever be able
to get the Irish people to co-operate with Great
Britain while partition remains. I wouldn't attempt it
myself, for I know I should fail.'

De Valera explained that he would be prepared to
allow Northern Ireland to retain its existing authority
provided that the powers vested in Westminster were
transferred to a central Irish parliament and that
there were 'adequate safeguards' to protect nationalists
in the area from the discrimination which they were
suffering at the time. He then followed up the inter-

view with appeals to the American Association for Recognition of the Irish Republic, the organisation that he had helped found while in the United States in 1920, and two of the ethnic newspapers that had consistently supported him, the New York *Irish World* and San Francisco *Leader*. He requested their help 'in making known to the American public the nature of partition and the wrong done by it to the Irish nation.'

Speaking in the Senate on 7 February 1939 the Taoiseach candidly admitted that he was launching a propaganda campaign against partition. He had ruled out force simply on the grounds that it would not be successful. 'I am not a pacifist by any means,' he explained, 'I would, if I could see a way of doing it effectively, rescue the people of Tyrone and Fermanagh, South Down, South Armagh, and Derry City from the coercion which they are suffering at the present, because I believe that, if there is to be no coercion that ought to apply all round.'

Since Chamberlain had privately admitted that he would like to see partition ended but could do nothing about it because of British public opinion, it was logical that de Valera should resort to propaganda in order — as he said himself — 'to instruct the British people'. There was no valid, moral justification for compelling contiguous nationalist areas to remain part of Northern Ireland. Even Frank MacDermot, who had the reputation of being an anglophile, observed that the boundary ought to be revised. He therefore asked if de Valera had ever requested the British to transfer the nationalist areas.

'I have not,' the Taoiseach replied, 'because I think the time has come when we ought to do the thing properly. That would only be a half measure.' In other words he was looking for all of the six counties or nothing. But how did he propose to get the area?

During a speech at the League of Nations in 1934 he actually suggested that the best solution of minority problems would be to transfer the minorities to their ancestral homes, where possible. He favoured a policy on the lines of a provision in the Treaty of Lausanne (1923) in accordance with which Greece and Turkey exchanged certain populations. If no other agreed solution could be found, he suggested that the Ulster question could be solved by transferring the Scottish-Irish Protestants from Northern Ireland to Britain and replacing them with a similar number of Roman Catholics of Irish extraction from Britain.

The Taoiseach made plans for a six-week visit to the United States in the spring of 1939 with the 'chief aim' of enlisting American public support for his campaign to end partition, but the visit had to be postponed because of a political crisis over the possible introduction of conscription in Northern Ireland. That was resolved by excluding the six counties from the conscription bill passed at Westminster, so the visit was rearranged for September, but it too had to be cancelled with the outbreak of war in Europe.

From de Valera's standpoint the postponements were most inopportune. He was at the height of his international prestige. As President of the League of Nations, he would have had a most impressive platform from which to appeal to Americans.

8

De Valera's Finest Hour

When the European War began in the autumn of 1939 de Valera's announcement that Ireland would remain neutral should have surprised no one. Ever since the failure of the League's sanctions against Italy, he had been emphasising that his government intended to remain aloof from the approaching conflict.

A number of factors undoubtedly contributed to the decision. The most important was probably the Taoiseach's belief that small countries should avoid involvement in major wars because they would neither be able to really influence the outcome nor would they carry much weight in drawing up the peace settlement. A second consideration was the realisation that remaining neutral would effectively demonstrate that in spite of existing ties with the British Commonwealth, the twenty-six counties constituted a completely independent state. The country's lack of adequate defences also had to be taken into consideration.

De Valera could have cited democratic principles as his justification for neutrality – since the overwhelming majority of the Irish people favoured staying out of the war. But he made it clear that this was not a reason, as far as he was concerned. 'It is not as representing the sentiment or feelings of our people that the government stands before you with this policy,' he told the Dáil on 2 September 1939. 'It stands before you as the guardian of the interests of our people, and it is to guard these interests as best we can that we are proposing to follow the policy.'

Even Edouard Hempel, the German Minister to Ireland, admitted that while the great majority of Irish people wanted to remain neutral, they nevertheless sympathised with the British. But the militant anglophobic minority represented by the IRA would undoubtedly have resisted any effort to align with Britain. Thus, if de Valera had wished to abandon neutrality, he could not have done so without risking civil strife. And he felt that 'for a divided people to fling itself into this war would be to commit suicide'.

Nevertheless the Taoiseach let the British know from the outset that he intended to pursue a neutrality that would be benevolently disposed towards them. He told Sir John Maffey, who took up the post of

British Representative to Ireland shortly after the war began, that he sympathised with Chamberlain for having 'done everything that a man could do to prevent this tragedy'. According to de Valera, the British leader's determined pursuit of peace, especially at Munich, had allowed the moral issues at stake in the war to be clearly defined. 'England has a moral position today', he said. 'Hitler might have his early successes, but the moral position would tell.'

The German Minister was certainly under no illusions about where de Valera's sympathies lay. In May 1940 he predicted that the Taoiseach would 'maintain the line of friendly understanding with England as far as it is at all possible', because of geographical and economic considerations 'as well as his democratic principles, even in the face of the threatening danger of Ireland becoming involved in the war.'

There was a limit, however, to the benevolence of Irish policy. De Valera was not prepared to endanger neutrality by allowing the British to use Irish bases, nor was he willing to accede to a British suggestion that a joint Anglo-Irish force should patrol the Irish coast, but he did come up with a scheme to help the British. Once Irish coast watchers located any German submarines or aircraft, the Taoiseach told Maffey that they would radio the information of its whereabouts. 'Not to you especially,' he explained. 'Your Admiralty must pick it up. We shall wireless it to the world. I will tell the German Minister of our intention to do this.'

In other words Irish defence forces would ostensibly be reporting to their headquarters on the activities of belligerents off the Irish coast, and each of the belligerents would be free to listen into the reports. Not that this would be of much help to the Germans, who would be too far from Ireland to use the information, but the British, on the other hand, would be near enough to act.

Dublin further demonstrated the benevolence of its neutrality in subsequent weeks by allowing some British boats to be stationed in Irish waters for air-sea rescue purposes and by turning over seven modern oil tankers to British registry. Irish authorities also agreed not to charter any neutral ships except through Britain so that Anglo-Irish competition for neutral shipping could be eliminated and chartering rates kept down.

During the early months of the war the Taoiseach was primarily concerned with domestic matters, especially the threat posed by the IRA's efforts to exploit Britain's difficulties. There was considerable public tension when some members of the IRA, who had been interned without trial, went on hunger strike to protest their confinement. Tension mounted as de Valera emphasised that none of the strikers would be freed, but he was dealt an embarrassing blow when the courts ruled that the government had acted unconstitutionally, so the strikers were released. This was soon followed by another setback in late December when the IRA raided the Magazine Fort in Phoenix Park and seized a considerable amount of arms and ammunition. But that raid proved to be a phyrric victory for the IRA, because most of the stolen material was not only quickly recovered, but the government used the disquiet caused by the raid to secure a speedy closure of the legal loopholes recently exploited in the courts.

De Valera was so concerned with domestic affairs that he declined to preside over an emergency session of the League of Nations, which had been called for December 1939 to discuss the Soviet Union's invasion of Finland. Efforts had been made to persuade him to go to Geneva on the grounds that he could secure colossal publicity by denouncing the Soviet invasion and by emphasising that morality among nations was still something to be reckoned with. But

he rejected the suggestion by pointing out that if he
[116] referred to what was happening in Finland, he would
also have to speak about Poland, Slovakia and such
areas invaded by the Nazis, which might then involve
Ireland in the war with Germany.

'There is no use in an oration at this time', the
Taoiseach said. In the foreseeable future the only
method of persuasion would not be with words, but
with 'tanks, bombs, and machine guns'. Concluding
with his voice shaking with agitation, he told the
American Minister that he felt 'like a man behind a
glass wall witnessing the destruction of everything he
held dear, but absolutely paralysed and impotent to
take any action to avert universal destruction.'

The Irish leader was certainly in an unenviable position. He could expect no international help for his
policy of maintaining neutrality. Even in the United
States, which did not formally enter the war until
December 1941, there was little sympathy in official
circles for Irish policy. In May 1940 when the Germans
invaded the Low Countries, for instance, de Valera
tried to get President Roosevelt to announce that the
United States was interested in the preservation of the
status quo in regard to Ireland, but the White House
was unwilling to make even that limited statement.

Just how serious the situation was at the time
became apparent on the very day that the State
Department transmitted Roosevelt's refusal. Irish
authorities discovered that the IRA had been har-
bouring a German spy. Though the spy escaped and
remained at large for more than a year, his papers
were seized. Among them was found information
about the disposition of Irish defences and an invasion plan in accordance with which the Germans
would invade Northern Ireland and announce that
they were liberating the area. They would then call
on Irish nationalists to assist them.

As the collusion between the IRA and the Germans

could afford Britain an excuse to invade Ireland in order to forestall a German invasion, de Valera sent an emissary to London to assure the British not only that their assistance would be sought if the Germans invaded but also to suggest that secret talks be held between the British and Irish military to draw up contingency plans to repel the Germans. Measures to bolster Irish defences were intensified as hundreds of suspected would-be German collaborators in the IRA were interned for the duration of the war. At the same time an intensive recruiting drive for the Irish army was launched, and the two major opposition parties in the Dáil were invited to join Fianna Fáil in establishing a National Defence Conference to advise the government on security matters.

De Valera went on radio on 1 June 1940 to warn of the dangers facing the country. 'When great powers are locked in mortal combat', he explained, 'the rights of small nations are as naught to them: the only thing that counts is how one may secure an advantage over the other, and, if the violation of our territory promises such an advantage, then our territory will be violated, our country will be made a cockpit, our homes will be levelled and our people slaughtered.'

For the next year there was a series of crises as Irish authorities feared that either British or German forces would invade. De Valera sought assurances from both governments that they would respect Irish neutrality. At first both refused, so he then played them off against each other. He made it clear to the British and German representatives that his government would invite help from the enemy of any country that invaded Ireland. He even told the Italian Minister in June 1940 that the discovery of the German spy had so shattered his confidence that in order to resist mounting pressure to hand over ports to Britain, he needed an assurance that the Axis powers would respect Irish sovereignty.

The British government, which had secretly decided
against seizing Irish bases, had recently been trying to
persuade the Taoiseach to give back the facilities
handed over in 1938. If Dublin would co-operate,
they offered to set up a commission to end partition.
The British proposal, which was made in the last
week of June 1940, was too vague to provide a firm
guarantee of Irish unity, but de Valera in any case
made it clear that even if such an assurance were
given, he would not bargain with neutrality. The only
solution, he said, would be for Northern Ireland to
withdraw from the war and agree to unity, then the
new united Irish parliament would consider declaring
war on Germany. He candidly warned, however that
such a declaration would probably be defeated, even
if he supported it himself.

At the time the Irish cabinet was divided between
those who favoured Britain and those who gave the
impression of sympathising with Berlin. Probably
none of them really favoured the Nazis, but they
were convinced that Germany was going to win the
war, so they were anxious to curry favour with the
German Minister. They were so nervous, according to
one of their colleagues, that they gave the impression
at cabinet meetings that Hempel might be looking
over their shoulders.

Events seemed to close in on de Valera in early
July 1940. Hitler was deliberately creating the
impression that Germany was about to invade Ireland,
and there were fears that Britain might lauch a pre-
emptive strike. Those fears were greatly exacerbated
when Irish authorities arrested a British officer collecting information to be used by British troops in
Ireland. On top of that Winston Churchill, who had
taken over as Prime Minister in May, was known to
believe that Irish ports were strategically important.
And he gave rise to considerable uneasiness by referring to the German threat to Ireland in the same

speech in which he justified attacking the French fleet in order to prevent it falling into German hands. As [119] Churchill had authorised the attack on ships of his recent ally, there could be little doubt that he would endorse drastic action to prevent the Germans getting hold of Irish ports.

The threat of inviting German assistance was hardly sufficient to keep the British at bay, seeing that there was a question of whether Germany was in a position to effectively help the Irish, so de Valera also sought to enlist the protection of American public opinion. He gave an interview to a correspondent of the *New York Times* in which he stressed that there was no intention of abandoning neutrality. His tactics were basically designed to remind the American people that — like themselves — the people of Ireland wished to avoid involvement in the war. As a result any British attack on Ireland would make Churchill look little better than Hitler and would probably thereby damage the popular support so necessary if the Roosevelt administration were to render effective aid to Britain.

De Valera's overall approach bore fruit on both fronts. Berlin ordered Hempel to assure the Irish government that Germany would respect Irish neutrality, and the Secretary of State in Washington cautioned the British Ambassador against any attack on Ireland. The Ambassador responded with an assurance that Britain would undertake no such venture unless the Germans attacked first, but British authorities were never prepared to give Dublin the same assurance.

In November 1940 Churchill caused further uneasiness in Ireland by initiating a propaganda campaign in the British and American press to persuade the Irish government to hand over the ports. Afraid that this was an effort to minimise the possible American reaction to a British violation of Irish neutrality, de Valera again appealed for American public support. He openly

called on Irish-Americans to start a campaign to drum
[120] up support for Irish neutrality. His request was quickly
greeted with vociferous support from organised Irish-
American elements.

The British, Canadian, and American representatives in Dublin all warned that the British propaganda
efforts were proving counter-productive, but Churchill
was not prepared to placate the Taoiseach's fears. 'I
think it would be better to let de Valera stew in his
own juice for a while', the Prime Minister wrote, adding that 'the less we say to de Valera at this juncture
the better, and certainly nothing must be said to
reassure him.'

The following month de Valera actually used the
continuing British threat to frustrate efforts to
increase the size of the German legation in Dublin. As
the British, who had no representative in Ireland
before the war, had been allowed to establish a diplomatic mission that was considerably larger than the
German one, the Taoiseach had to accede when the
Germans insisted on being allowed to introduce additional staff, but he demanded that the diplomats
would have to arrive by a normal commercial route.
He would not allow them to come by special plane,
nor be dropped by parachute, because he said that
this would afford Britain a pretext for charging that
there was some kind of collusion between Dublin and
Berlin. It was only afterwards that Hempel learned to
his dismay that he had been outwitted. All commercial transportation to Ireland stopped in Britain first
which, of course, effectively killed the plans for additional staff. Yet one crisis was hardly over when there
were signs that another was beginning.

Within a matter of days the British began exerting
economic pressure on the Dublin government by
terminating their agreement to afford a certain amount
of shipping space to the Irish in return for the agreement not to charter neutral ships. The British were

acting within their rights, but certainly not within the spirit of their agreement. By then they had most of the available neutral shipping under contract, and they estimated that Ireland would only be able to secure enough ships to fulfil about a quarter of her needs. The Irish government was therefore compelled to introduce rationing, coupled with compulsory tillage to ensure that the country produced sufficient food for her own people.

In April 1941 the horrors of war came perilously close when more than a thousand people were killed in two bombing raids on Belfast. De Valera reacted by ordering fire brigades in the twenty-six counties to help fight the fires in Belfast. It was undoubtedly an unneutral act to render such assistance, but then the Taoiseach claimed legal sovereignty over the area.

The whole partition issue threatened to erupt the following month when Churchill announced that Westminster was considering extending compulsory military service to Northern Ireland. The nationalist minority in the North reacted predictably by objecting vociferously to Churchill's proposal, so de Valera, who feared civil strife throughout the island, instructed the Irish High Commissioner in London to try to persuade the British leader to abandon the idea. When this failed, he turned to the Americans and Canadians for assistance. Roosevelt and Prime Minister Mackenzie King of Canada both responded by making strong representations against the extention of conscription, as did the Australian Prime Minister and most members of the British cabinet. Churchill was therefore compelled to abandon the idea. Serious difficulties had undoubtedly been averted.

But there was the starkest reminder yet of the dangers still facing the Irish people later the same week when an apparently disorientated German plane bombed Dublin, killing over thirty people and injuring scores of others. Nevertheless the real danger to Ireland virtually disappeared a few weeks later when German forces invaded the Soviet Union.

Some of the war's more decisive battles had yet to be fought but – as long as the Soviet Union kept the Germans engaged, which of course turned out to be for the duration of the war – the Irish government could afford to breathe relatively easily. In March 1943, for instance, when the Battle of the Atlantic was at its height and Britain was faced with what her naval historians have described as her most serious crisis of the war, the situation in Ireland was such that de Valera delivered a St Patrick's Day address in which he described conditions that could hardly have contrasted more starkly with what was happening in the war-torn countries of the continent. Declaring the restoration of the Gaelic language as the most important issue facing the nation, he went on to depict the kind of Ireland he wanted. It would, he said, not only be a united Gaelic-speaking island, but 'a land whose countryside would be bright with cozy homesteads, whose fields and villages would be joyous with the sounds of industry, with the romping of sturdy children, the contests of athletic youths, the laughter of comely maidens, whose firesides would be forums for the wisdom of serene old age. It would, in a word, be the home of a people living the life that God desires that man should live.'

As the Axis threat to Ireland receded the Taoiseach showed a growing disposition to help the Allies. When the United States formally entered the conflict in late 1941 he even risked German anger by publicly announcing that Ireland would adopt a benevolent neutrality towards the Americans. The Canadian High Commissioner in Dublin certainly had no doubt about de Valera's sincerity. 'It has been demonstrated', he explained, 'that the Irish government will do almost anything to help us short of involving themselves in the war.' But the Americans did not appreciate the situation at the time because, for one thing, they were unaware of the extent of secret Anglo-Irish co- operation. When David Gray, the American Minister, learned some weeks later, he was genuinely surprised. He reported that the co-operation, which had de Valera's full blessing, had been 'beyond what might reasonably have been believed possible'.

The same co-operation was then extended to the Americans. While German airmen who came down in the twenty-six counties were interned at the Curragh, hundreds of their American counterparts were spirited over the border into Northern Ireland. De Valera even agreed not to intern Allied pilots who landed in Ireland while on non-operational flights such as training missions, or while testing equipment. According to Churchill's son, Randolph, the whole arrangement was simply 'a convenient fiction' to allow Dublin to help the Allies while preserving the appearance of neutrality.

But the American Minister was not satisfied. He was annoyed that Irish neutrality seemed to hurt the Allies in two ways – by denying them vital bases and by allowing Axis diplomats to remain in Ireland, thereby affording them a chance to spy on the Allies. Moreover he was further annoyed by de Valera's blatant appeal for American public support over the head of the Roosevelt administration, and he was infuriated in January 1942 when the Taoiseach – irritated that the United States had ignored the Dublin government's claim to sovereignty over Northern Ireland by stationing American troops in the area without consulting him – issued a statement alluding to the American troops as an army of occupation. Yet de Valera had not protested some months earlier when the Germans violated the same supposed sovereignty by bombing Belfast.

What troubled Gray most, however, was a suspicion that the Irish leader would try to inject the partition question into postwar American politics by inciting Irish-Americans to use their influence in an effort to get Washington to insist that partition be ended as part of the postwar peace settlement. He was afraid that de Valera might undermine American support for the future peace settlement just as he had helped to wreck the Versailles Treaty back in 1919. Gray therefore decided to try to discredit de Valera by getting him on record as refusing to help the Allies. His initial proposal was that President Roosevelt should ask Dublin to break off diplomatic relations with the Axis powers and abandon neutrality. But authorities in both Washington and London opposed that proposal. They did not think that Ireland could contribute to their war effort in any significant way so they objected to taking any chance of the Taoiseach complying with the request. They noted, for example, that even the bases that Churchill had made such a fuss over would be of little use. Ever since the Germans got control of the French coast in 1940 the shipping routes off the south coast of Ireland – for which southern ports had provided strategic protection during World War I – were too exposed and were no longer of use because Allied shipping had to take the safer route by Northern Ireland, where the Allies already had bases. Consequently Ireland's accession to the Allies cause would actually have hurt the war effort, because the Allies would have become morally obliged to divert men and equipment to protect not only useless facilities but also virtually undefended Irish cities.

The American Minister next proposed that Washington simply ask de Valera to expel Axis representatives from Ireland on the grounds that they were an espionage threat to Allied preparations for the invasion of Europe in 1944. While that proposal was being considered in Washington, the British acted on their own and informally requested that de Valera confiscate a radio transmitter in the German legation. This was done, so de Valera was furious two months later when, without making any informal representations, the American delivered a formal diplomatic note asking 'as an absolute minimum' that Axis representatives be expelled from Ireland. He immediately rejected the request.

Next day the British delivered a note supporting the American request. The Taoiseach expressed annoyance that in spite of the secret co-operation that he had given when approached informally in the past, the Allies had delivered formal notes without making any informal representations beforehand. He therefore contended that the notes were just a scheme to push Ireland into the war and thus rob the country of the symbols of her independence. 'It was obvious', Maffey reported, 'that he attached immense importance to this symbolic factor.'

When news of the Irish refusal broke, it made front-page headlines throughout the United States. There followed a great smear campaign against Irish neutrality in the American press, which depicted de Valera as a Nazi sympathiser. In the emotive atmosphere many newspapers actually called for economic or military sanctions against Ireland.

To public opinion in Ireland the whole affair seemed like an effort to force the country into the war, so de Valera's refusal was seen as a determined defence of neutrality, which undoubtedly had the support of the overwhelming majority of the people. He was therefore able to use the whole affair to his own political advantage by calling a general election in May 1944. Fianna Fáil, which had lost its overall majority in the Dáil the previous autumn, gained fourteen seats in the ensuing election to give the party one of the most comfortable majorities in its history. Nevertheless de Valera's international image had been seriously tarnished by all the unfavourable publicity. Gray had certainly achieved his own primary objective of discrediting the Irish leader in the United States.

De Valera further discredited himself the following year, at the end of the war, by visiting the German legation to express condolence following the death of Hitler. Even in Ireland the expression of sympathy for the death of the Führer was widely resented. The Taoiseach had apparently been goaded into the action by his annoyance at Gray, who only the previous day had lectured him about having a moral responsibility to set aside both the niceties of neutrality and the sanctity of the German legation. Gray had argued unsuccessfully to be allowed to seize the German legation before Berlin formally surrendered so that any documents that the legation staff might wish to destroy could be captured.

No doubt de Valera was still annoyed the following day when he learned of Hitler's death. Having paid a moving tribute in the Dáil and proffered his condolence to Gray following Roosevelt's death little over a fortnight earlier, the Taoiseach felt that it be an insult to Hempel if strict protocol were ignored in Hitler's case. And the Irish leader was obviously not about to insult Hempel, for whom he had a much higher regard than for Gray.

'During the whole of the war,' de Valera wrote, 'Dr Hempel's conduct was irreproachable. He was always friendly and invariably correct — in marked contrast with Gray. I certainly was not going to add to his humiliation in the hour of defeat.'

Churchill, who admitted to having 'followed Gray's lead' in the scheme to discredit the Taoiseach the previous year, apparently saw a chance to secure publicity that would further undermine support for de Valera's expected attempt to end partition. In a victory broadcast on 13 May 1945 the British leader contrasted the help that the Allies had received from Northern Ireland with the Dublin government's 'deadly blow' in refusing to allow Britain to use bases in the twenty-six counties. 'Had it not been for the loyalty and friend- ship of Northern Ireland', he declared, 'we should have been forced to come to close quarters with Mr de Valera or perish for ever from the earth.' He added that Britain simply 'left the de Valera government to frolic with the German and later with the Japanese representatives to their heart's content.'

Three days later the Taoiseach recouped all the political ground that he had lost at home following Hitler's death by delivering a statesmanlike response to Churchill's outburst. It was probably the most effective speech of his long career. Somewhat condescendingly, he explained that allowances could be made for the British leader's remarks on the grounds that they had been made on an emotional occasion, but he continued:

> Mr Churchill makes it clear that, in certain circumstances, he would have violated our neutrality and that he would justify his action by Britain's necessity. It seems strange to me that Mr Churchill does not see that this, if accepted, would mean that Britain's necessity would become a moral code and that when this necessity became sufficiently great, other people's rights were not to count.
>
> It is quite true that other great powers believe in this same code — in their own regard — and have behaved in accordance with it. That is precisely why we have the disastrous succession of wars — World War No. 1 and World War No. 2 — and shall it be World War No. 3?

De Valera went on to commend the Prime Minister for not succumbing to the temptation to violate Irish neutrality. 'By resisting his temptation in this instance', the Taoiseach said, 'Mr Churchill, instead of adding another horrid chapter to the already bloodstained record of relations between England and this country, has advanced the cause of international morality an important step.'

The address was regarded as a masterpiece in Ireland. Even people who had long eyed de Valera with suspicion were thrilled with his speech. He had capped off his adroit handling of the country's difficulties during the trying years of the Second World War with a masterful reply to one of his government's bitterest critics.

Although the war was over, there were still some loose ends to be cleared up. In June 1945 the Allies asked Dublin to hand over all German internees, spies and diplomats. But de Valera refused to repatriate either the diplomats or the spies, and he insisted that he would only turn over the 250 internees if first given an assurance that none would be executed or handed to the Soviets. The British agreed to those stipulations, so the internees were given to them. Some protracted negotiations followed before Dublin also agreed to hand over the spies. But when one of them killed himself, the deportation order on another was rescinded because he too had threatened to commit suicide.

There was no move, however, to release the hundreds of IRA people interned. Soon demands for their release became a hot political issue. Of course, those internees could easily have secured their own release by simply swearing to have nothing further to do with the IRA, but very few of them were prepared to take such an oath.

9

The Twilight Years

Much of the campaign for the release of the Republican internees was orchestrated by a new political party, Clann na Poblachta, which began making serious inroads into Fianna Fáil's political support among both Republican and radical elements. Many of the Republicans who had voted for Fianna Fáil in the twenties and thirties had long since become disenchanted, as had a number of radicals.

Joseph Connolly, a prominent member of the first Fianna Fáil government, had become particularly disillusioned over the Taoiseach's unwillingness to pursue radical land reforms. 'In my later talks with de Valera,' he wrote, 'I formed the opinion that he no longer welcomed discussion much less criticism, and that what he wanted beside him was a group of "yes-men" who agreed with everything and anything the party (with himself as leader) approved.'[33]

It would really have been an extremely difficult time for any government. The winter of 1946—47 was one of the severest on record, and it was complicated by a serious energy crisis brought about by a drastic cutback on coal supplies from Britain. As a result transportation was seriously disrupted and an already chronic shortage of raw materials was exacerbated, forcing many industries to close and causing widespread redundancies. On top of that, Fianna Fáil was rocked by a number of scandals. Moreover the party was obviously making no headway towards Irish unity, which was supposedly its primary objective.

There was actually a great deal of confusion over the country's status and its relationship with the British Commonwealth. Nobody seemed quite sure whether or not Ireland was a member of the Commonwealth. De Valera deliberately evaded the question. When pressed for an answer in July 1945, for instance, he simply responded that 'in all political systems there are relationships that it is wiser to leave undefined'. Clann na Poblachta took an unambiguous stand in favour of an all-Ireland republic. So the Fianna Fáil leader had to protect his own Republican wing by becoming more specific. 'Twenty-six of our counties are a republic,' he told a Dublin gathering in October 1947, and if the Irish nation continued to give Fianna Fáil support, the party would have 'a better chance of securing the whole of Ireland as a republic than any other party.' But Clann na Poblachta's impressive growth continued as it won two Dáil by-elections the following month. Some people equated those successes with the Sinn Féin by-election victories of 1917, and there were even predictions that the new party would emulate the Sinn Féin showing of 1918 in the next general election. In an obvious move to deny the party further time to organise itself properly, the Taoiseach called a surprise general election for February 1948, even though the existing Dáil, with its safe Fianna Fáil majority, still had some fifteen months to run.

During the election campaign de Valera declared that he was ready to take up his anti-partition efforts where they had been interrupted by the Second World War. He announced that he would go to the United States to drum up American support and that he would also appeal to other countries for help. 'I promise,' he declared in Sligo, 'that the pressure of public opinion of the Irish race, not in Ireland only, but throughout the world, will be concentrated on this question'. He added that he also intended to enlist the support of 'public opinion not only of those who have Irish blood in their veins, but of their fellow citizens – men and women – of other races'.

Over the years Fianna Fáil had obviously grown conservative as there was little of the promise of new

radical programmes that the party had held out during the 1930s. De Valera actually seemed satisfied
with the social progress already made. In fact, shortly
after the election, he declared in Ennis that there was
'probably not in the whole world at the present a
country in which there is such a decent standard of
living as there is in this part of Ireland.' The Fianna
Fáil leader managed to exude such an air of sincerity
that he imbued an enormous number of people with
an intense loyalty to himself – so much so that the
party's most popular slogan was simply, 'Up Dev.'
To what extent his election tactics were successful must remain a matter for conjecture. Fianna Fáil
easily won enough seats to remain the largest party in
the Dáil, while Clann na Poblachta, which won only
ten seats, suffered irreparable damage to its momentum. But, Fianna Fáil lost its majority and John A.
Costello of Fine Gael was elected Taoiseach at the
head of a coalition government.

In spite of that setback de Valera still went ahead
with his planned visit to the United States. The trip,
which lasted for four weeks, took in various American
cities, including Washington, D.C., where he had what
he characterised as 'just a friendly chat' with President Harry Truman. Other stops included New York,
San Francisco, Los Angeles, Chicago, Detroit, Philadelphia, and Boston. The Fianna Fáil leader explained
that he had come to thank Americans for their past
assistance in the struggle for Irish independence and
to request further help.

In some respects his attitude towards the Irish
question in relation to the overall international
situation was relatively similar to that of almost three
decades earlier. Just as he had been critical of Ireland's
exclusion from the League of Nations in 1919, he
now criticised the fact that the country was being
denied membership of the United Nations by the veto
of the Soviet Union. He therefore predicted that the

new organisation would not be any more effective than its predecessor. 'I had more hope of the success of the League of Nations than of the United Nations', he said. Of course the real focus of de Valera's criticism was not the United Nations but the British, because of their role in Northern Ireland. 'They tell you that what they call Ulster must not be coerced, he said in Boston. 'Answer them that it is being coerced, that the majority of the people of four of the cut-off counties and the great minority in the rest are being held in territory garrisoned by British arms against their own wishes to unite with the rest of Ireland.'

'If what is happening in partitioned Ireland today were being done in Eastern Europe by Russia,' he added, 'the people on whom it was being done would be entitled to ask assistance, and many who talk of democracy now would cry out against the injustice.' He charged that Britain was acting more undemocratically than the Soviet Union, because the British were partitioning Ireland in the name of democracy, while he contended that the Russians just acted blatantly without any pretence of worthy motives.

'If I were Stalin, and wanted what Stalin wanted,' the Fianna Fáil leader explained, 'I would imitate Britain and get away with it as Britain is getting away with it. It would be easy to pick an area somewhere in Europe with a communist majority and, on pretence of safeguarding a minority, to cut off that area, and make it appear as if it were being governed by a majority.'

In seeking justice he tried to portray himself as being willing to lean over backwards to satisfy the Unionists in Northern Ireland by being prepared to allow them to keep Stormont with its existing powers. But if they were not ready to accept such a compromise, he said that they should be bought out. 'We would say to them,' he explained, 'we would prefer that you stay, but if you prefer an outside power we cannot have our unity threatened by your loyalty. If you don't want to be Irish, we are prepared to let you go and compensate you.' He was still apparently thinking of his pre-war plan of transferring Northern Ireland Protestants to Britain and replacing them with Roman Catholics of Irish extraction from Britain.

Following the American tour, de Valera went to Australia, where he stayed for six weeks repeatedly denouncing partition and Britain's responsibility for it. Then after a four-day stay in New Zealand, he returned home with brief stops in Ceylon, Burma, and in India, where he met with Prime Minister Pandit Nehru and his daughter, Indira Gandhi. Next he stopped in Rome for a meeting with the Italian Premier, Alcide de Gasperi, before visiting the Vatican for an audience with Pope Pius XII and his acting Secretary of State, Monsignor Giovani Montini (later Pope Paul VI).

De Valera returned to Dublin in time for the Fianna Fáil Ard Fheis, at which he announced that he had made arrangements for anti-partition campaigns in the United States, Australia, and New Zealand, and hoped that similar efforts could also be organised in Canada, South Africa, and India. 'We have a splendid case,' he said. 'Partition is on a rotten foundation and it will totter and end. All we want to do is make up our mind to make the proper assault.'

Since being forced into opposition the Fianna Fáil leader had been showing distinct signs of hardening his attitude toward partition. Some people suggested that this was simply because he had been relieved of the responsibility of office and could speak out with blatant disregard for the international consequences. They asked why he had not spoken out in such a manner while in office.

'The reason is,' de Valera responded, 'that we have been doing things in regular order.' He believed that it would only be possible to end partition once the issue had been isolated. After the other outstanding issues

had been settled in 1938, he had indeed begun making preparations for a drive to end partition, but his efforts were wrecked by the outbreak of hostilities in Europe.

It would have been futile to seek international support for an anti-partition campaign during the war, especially in the United States, where interest in ethnic affairs virtually ceased following the country's entry into the conflict in 1941. The Irish-Americans felt that ethnic considerations should be put aside so that they could devote their full attention to prosecuting the war. As a result Irish considerations were temporarily forgotten, but by late 1947 there were signs of a resurgence of Irish-American interest in ethnic affairs with the staging of Ireland's premier sporting event, the All-Ireland Gaelic Football Final, in New York, and the formation of a new organisation, the American League for an Undivided Ireland, which aimed at organising American opinion against partition.

Nevertheless the international efforts that de Valera spoke about at the Fianna Fáil Ard Fheis never really amounted to much. The American campaign, for example, failed to excite much interest outside the Irish-American community. For one thing other Americans were generally disillusioned with what they had been led to believe was de Valera's indifferent neutrality — in marked contrast with that of Northern Ireland, which had not only provided bases but also had welcomed American troops. Moreover Americans could hardly have supported the scheme for the transfer of populations. After all, Protestants in Northern Ireland could trace their roots in the area back to the early seventeenth century, with the result that calling for their removal would be like asking most Americans to leave the United States in order to give the country back to the Indians.

On the whole, therefore, the efforts to enlist international support were ill-conceived, especially as there was no indication that the hostility to unity was waning in Northern Ireland. In fact, Irish neutrality seemed to have psychologically widened the political gulf between Belfast and Dublin, and the latter made little effort to alleviate the legitimate fears that the Northern majority had about Irish unity. Over the years the Dublin government had effectively helped to perpetuate the desire for partition by failing to demonstrate a real spirit of tolerance or broadmindedness. For example, there was discrimination in the twenty-six counties against Protestant values in such matters as divorce, contraception and censorship. Moreover, de Valera himself was involved in a celebrated incident in 1931 when people in Co. Mayo objected to the appointment of a librarian simply because she was a Protestant. As leader of the opposition, he contended in the Dáil that the people of Mayo, who were overwhelmingly Roman Catholic, were 'justified in insisting upon a Catholic librarian'. After taking over the leadership of the country he and his colleagues made the mistake of implying, according to John H. Whyte's *Church and State in Modern Ireland,* that 'the only true Irishmen were Catholics', but in fairness to him, he 'did not act on the doctrines which he had propounded in the Mayo library debate'. In fact, he was instrumental in having the founder of the Gaelic League, Douglas Hyde, who happened to be a Protestant, selected as the first President of Ireland under the constitution of 1937.

Although Fianna Fáil did not institute the discrimination against Protestant values, this was actually intensified while the party was in power. Divorce — hitherto illegal — was made unconstitutional, while a ban on the advertising of contraceptives was extended to both their sale and importation. In addition, censorship was carried to really absurd lengths, especially during the war years. The *Irish Times,* which was then still closely identified with the Protestant community, [136] was prevented from running an announcement regarding Sunday services at Kingstown Presbyterian Church, because that church had refused to change its name after the town of Kingstown had been named Dun Laoghaire. The censorial attitude extended even to radio programmes, as Radio Éireann banned jazz and the records of Bing Crosby because it was felt that these would have an undesirable effect on the Irish people. It is unlikely that de Valera was directly responsible for specific excesses of the censorship, except to the extent that he was leader of the government which had power to prevent such occurences. The editor of the *Irish Times,* which suffered some particularly heavy-handed treatment from the censors during the war, wrote privately at the time that whenever he appealed to de Valera, which was quite often, he 'found the long fellow more than anxious to be fair'.[34]

It would be wrong to suggest that Northern Protestants were opposed to Irish unity simply because of discrimination against their values by the Dublin government. Had there been no discrimination, the overwhelming majority would undoubtedly have still been opposed to ending partion, if only on emotional grounds. They were no more willing to enter a united Ireland than the people of the rest of the island were prepared to go back into the United Kingdom.

The real significance of the Southern discrimination, therefore, was that, in the eyes of Northern Unionists, it provided strong evidence that they would be discriminated against in a united Ireland. In a thoughtful biography of de Valera, published in 1939, Seán Ó Faoláin wrote that 'No Northerner can possibly like such features of Southern life as at present constituted, as its pervasive clerical control; its censorship; its Gaelic revival; its isolationist economic policy. De Valera realises the effect of at least some of these things. He shows no readiness to relax any of them.'

The economic nationalism pursued by the Fianna [137] Fáil government during the 1930s would have had a disastrous effect on the North's industrialised economy, which was heavily dependent on the British market. At the same time Northerners looked with disquiet on the efforts to revive the Gaelic language. For example, there was institutionalised discrimination within the Civil Service and educational system in favour of those able to use the language. In addition, de Valera actually declared on several occasions that he would prefer the restoration of the language to Irish freedom or the ending of partition. 'If I had to make a choice between political freedom without the language, and the language without political freedom,' he declared on one such occasion, 'I would choose the latter. For that freedom which a nation loses can be regained, but a language once it is dead can never be revived.' Unionists in Northern Ireland, who had no affection for Gaelic, could hardly be blamed for concluding that in a united Ireland de Valera might take away their freedom, if they refused to use the language.

He certainly showed no inclination to compromise in regard to the Gaelic revival or the question of Republicanism. 'I do not see why,' he declared in 1947, 'the people of this part of Ireland should sacrifice ideals which they hold dear — completely sacrifice those ideals in order to meet the views of people whose position fundamentally is not as just or as right as our position is.' He added that the existing External Association with the Commonwealth was 'the farthest we could go to meet their views in the North'.

The coalition government, which succeeded Fianna Fáil, took an even more hardline approach, as it formally withdrew from the Commonwealth by repealing the External Relations Act and formally declaring the twenty-six counties to be the Republic of Ireland

in 1949. Although that declaration was psycho-
logically a momentous occasion, it was not very important from the practical standpoint, seeing that de Valera had long ago fulfilled the promise he had made in April 1933 to dismantle the 1921 Treaty to such an extent that the declaration of a Republic would only be a mere formality. He did not therefore raise any objection to the repeal of the External Relations Act.

The coalition also invited de Valera to an all-party conference at the Mansion House on 27 January 1949, with a view to organising a campaign to end partition. The fanfare with which the anti-partition drive was launched was probably the strongest show of solidarity between the Irish political parties since the Mansion House Conference of 1918 had opposed the extension of conscription during the First World War.

Anti-partition rallies were held in various English cities. Attending several of those gatherings, de Valera repeatedly stressed that the areas of the six counties in which there were nationalist majorities should be handed over to the Dublin government, but he did not pretend that he would be satisfied with such a settlement. It would obviously be only a step towards his ultimate goal.

'We demand that these counties where there is an overwhelming majority against partition should be given back to us in all fairness and justice,' he told a rally in Newcastle in February 1949. 'But that would not solve the partition problem, because our ancient homeland would be severed and multilated.' In Northern Ireland elections the previous week anti-partition candidates had a majority of 52.86 per cent in Co. Fermanagh, and 52.5 per cent in Co. Tyrone.

In calling for the transfer of those areas, or re-partition as it was called, de Valera was pursuing a different approach than that he had followed in office. Then he had not asked for nationalist territory because he thought that the whole partition problem should be solved at the same time. The coalition government later pursued essentially the same line. On visiting London for talks in March 1949, for instance, Seán MacBride, the Minister for External Affairs, stated that the Dublin government could not favour being given only the areas with nationalist majorities. He explained that he was relying on the principle that Ireland was a single unit. No doubt MacBride was afraid that if the nationalist areas were taken from the six counties, then the nationalist minority in what would remain of Northern Ireland would be too small to pose a really significant force for Irish unity, with the result that the prospects for complete national independence might be irreparably damaged. In short, it seemed that successive Dublin governments were content that the nationalist people in such areas as Fermanagh, Tyrone, South Down, South Armagh, and Derry City should in effect be left as hostages in the hope that they would eventually help secure Irish unity.

The Costello government continued with a similar foreign policy to de Valera. The popular irritation over the existence of partition was cited as the reason for refusing to join either the North Atlantic Treaty Organisation, or a suggested European federation: de Valera agreed with both decisions. He told the Assembly of the Council of Europe in Strasbourg in August 1949, for example, that it would be very difficult to persuade the Irish people to enter a European federation at the time. 'I am sure,' he said, 'you can understand with what a cynical smile an Irish citizen would regard you if you spoke to him about uniting into a huge state unit the several states of Europe with their diverse national traditions so long as he contemplates his own country kept divided against his will.'

But the Fianna Fáil leader made it clear that he

was not personally opposed to the idea of a united
Europe. 'If the nations here on the mainland of the
continent consider that they cannot wait for us,' he
added, 'perhaps they should consider going on without us by an agreement for a close union among
themselves. It is from no desire to interfere with or
delay them that some of us here have spoken against
the attempt at immediate federation. It is simply
because we know the task that would confront us in
persuading our people to proceed by that road.'

As international tension mounted with the outbreak of war in Korea, de Valera's attitude seemed to
be the same as during the crises immediately prior to
the Second World War. 'As long as the evil of partition exists,' he told a London gathering, 'a divided
Ireland would have no option but to remain neutral
in a third world war.' By implication he seemed to be
holding out the possibility of co-operation if Irish
unity were secured. But when asked if he would agree
to participating in such a war if partition were ended,
he replied — as he had so often before — that it would
not be possible to make any commitment in advance.
'If you attempt to condition freedom,' he said, 'you
have not got it.'

The only concession that he was prepared to offer
Northern Ireland was the same one that he had been
talking about for the past thirty years. He would agree
to Stormont retaining its existing powers, provided
those were applied impartially and the powers vested
in Westminster were transferred to an all-Ireland parliament. He stressed, however, that there could be no
question of the majority in the six counties remaining British. 'If they want to be Irish we will receive
them with a heart and a half,' he said. 'But they must
choose either to be Irish or British. They can't be
both.'

Within a few weeks the Costello government fell
over a squabble that developed within the coalition,

after the Roman Catholic hierarchy demanded that a health bill, known as the Mother and Child Scheme, be amended. When Noel Browne, the minister in charge, refused to alter the bill, he was forced to resign. He then published his correspondence with the bishops on the whole affair, resulting in political crisis that brought down the government. If the Northern majority had previously lacked firm evidence of what Ó Faoláin had described as the 'pervasive clerical control' in the twenty-six counties, then this controversy surely provided it, especially when the Taoiseach complained that the whole affair was supposed to have been settled behind closed doors.

In the ensuing general election Fianna Fáil gained only one seat, but this was enough for it to form a minority government with the help of a number of independent deputies, among them Noel Browne. De Valera, in his sixty-ninth year, again became Taoiseach, but he did not take on the portfolio of External Affairs. He was obviously slowing down and his eyes were giving him serious trouble. In fact, he was forced to spend several months in the Netherlands while a famous Utrecht oculist tried to save his deteriorating eyesight. The Taoiseach underwent six operations before returning home in late 1952, virtually blind except for some slight peripheral vision.

In the meantime his government had been confronted with a serious financial crisis which led to some stringent deflationary measures. As a result the Irish economy slowed down and unemployment increased, as did the number of emigrants leaving the country. For a time Fianna Fáil also seemed likely to become embroiled in a controversy with the Roman Catholic hierarchy when James Ryan, the Minister for Health, moved for the implementation of the Mother and Child Scheme. The hierarchy wrote an open letter to the press condemning the legislation, but de Valera and Ryan avoided an open confrontation by hurridly going north to meet Cardinal D'Alton in Drogheda, where certain modifications to the bill were agreed upon. The hierarchy then withdrew its letter before actual publication, but too many people had seen the document for the matter to remain secret for long. The whole affair was another example of the enormous influence which the Roman Catholic hierarchy had in public life in the Republic of Ireland. It would certainly not have helped any effort to revive the anti-partition campaign, but in any case the Fianna Fáil government showed no such inclination. In fact, de Valera actually criticised the campaign that had been conducted by his predecessors.

If the coalition government had been serious about ending partition, he told a meeting in Drogheda on 28 February 1954, the British ambassador would have been expelled and all trade with Britain severed. Of course the Taoiseach did not advocate such a policy himself. He simply contended that a more moderate approach was needed. 'There is one policy which we can pursue,' he said, 'a policy of trying to establish decent relations between the people of Britain and the six counties and ourselves.' He added that partition should not be made a political issue. 'I don't want to make partition a political issue', he said, 'because I do not believe there is any one of the parties who have got the solution for it.' It was noteworthy that when he visited Britain for St Patrick's Day a couple of weeks later, he stressed the need for good Anglo-Irish relations, and played down the partition question.

The Irish people were obviously more concerned about the chronic unemployment and mass emigration. As Fianna Fáil did not have sufficient strength in the Dáil to really tackle these, de Valera called another general election in 1954. But it resulted in Fianna Fáil losses and the formation of another coalition under Costello's leadership.

In view of the earlier campaign against partition, it was not surprising that some members of the younger generation should become disillusioned with the apparent cynicism of politicians on the issue, so the IRA was able to stage a revival from the near disastrous effects of its wartime contacts with the Nazis. Buoyed by fresh blood, the organisation began a bombing campaign in Northern Ireland.

De Valera, who had met privately and tried to discourage IRA leaders before the bombing began, publicly denounced the violence at the Fianna Fáil Ard Fheis in November 1955. He stated that Irish unity 'could not be achieved by the exercise of force.' And he added that 'even if it were militarily successful we would not have the harmony essential' for real unity.

When the coalition tried to move against the IRA, however, Clann na Poblachta withdrew its vital support in the Dáil and tabled a motion of no confidence. Faced with imminent defeat the coalition government dissolved and a general election was called for February 1957. This time de Valera campaigned strenuously on the need for a strong government to tackle the country's problems, especially its continuing economic ills. The result was a resounding victory for Fianna Fáil, which secured a majority of nine seats. Although the party had gained larger majorities in 1938 and 1944, the seventy-nine seats won in 1957 were the highest total ever held by the party during de Valera's lifetime.

The new Fianna Fáil government lost little time in acting decisively. It re-introduced internment of IRA suspects and the level of violence in Northern Ireland soon showed a marked decline. The government also took what would eventually prove to be a most far reaching step on the road to economic growth by publishing the Whitaker Report, which called for drastic revisions in the earlier economic policies pursued by Fianna Fáil and the coalition governments. In the following years the implementation of the report virtually revolutionised the Irish economy. In January 1959 the Taoiseach told a meeting of the Fianna Fáil parliamentary party of his decision to retire from active politics in the near future. He explained that he intended to resign early enough to enable his successor and the party itself to prepare plans for the next election. He obviously had personal hopes of succeeding to the Presidency himself as the occupant of that office was due to retire shortly at the end of his second term. Explaining that he had been approached about running for the Presidency, de Valera announced that he would leave the 'matter completely in the hands of the party'. Of course, the party duly obliged by selecting him as its candidate.

Before formally retiring from active politics, however, de Valera wanted to tackle one last major issue. He was anxious to reform the electoral system, which he believed had been responsible for the instability of the past decade. He therefore proposed that the system of Proportional Representation (PR) be abolished. He got a bill through the Dáil to hold a constitutional referendum, which was scheduled for the same day as the Presidential election.

The results of the balloting were mixed from de Valera's viewpoint. He easily defeated his Fine Gael opponent for the presidency, but the attempt to abolish PR was soundly defeated.

On 25 June 1959 de Valera was inaugurated as President. His duties were mainly ceremonial during his fourteen years of office. He welcomed numerous heads of state, among them the Presidents of India, Pakistan, Zambia and the United States. The visit of President John F. Kennedy in 1963 was a particularly emotive occasion. When the American President was assassinated a few months later, de Valera undertook the arduous task of attending the funeral in Washington. It was one of many sad duties that he was to fulfil during his tenure, as several of his old cabinet [145] colleagues died, including his successor as Taoiseach, Séan Lemass.

There were also happier moments such as representing the Irish people at the coronation of Pope Paul VI and a state visit to the United States at the invitation of President Lyndon B. Johnson in 1964. It was forty-five years since he had gone to the United States seeking American recognition. Now he was returning as President of the internationally recognised Republic of Ireland, and he was honoured by being invited to address a joint session of Congress. It was a splendid occasion, as the blind eighty-one-year-old President delivered an effective twenty-five minute address without any notes to guide him.

In 1966 he attended various ceremonies commemorating the fiftieth anniversary of the Easter Rebellion. Even though his predecessor, Seán T. O'Kelly, had not been challenged for a second term in 1952, de Valera was too controversial a figure to be accorded such an honour. Fine Gael nominated T. F. O'Higgins to oppose him in 1966. While de Valera did not campaign actively, he was still narrowly re-elected, but not without some controversy. As he had decided not to campaign, the national radio and television service decided not to cover his opponent's campaign, which was somewhat unfair because de Valera was able to secure publicity though his official duties — not to mention the enormous exposure that he had received on television during the recent golden jubilee celebrations.

The noteworthy events of de Valera's second term included the country's entry into the European Economic Community and the election of a coalition government headed by the son of his old political opponent, W. T. Cosgrave. But it was affairs relating to the troubles in Northern Ireland which took centre stage in Irish politics during his final years. In August 1969 he actually played a major role in resolving a political crisis within Fianna Fáil when Kevin Boland resigned from the cabinet in protest over the government's policy regarding Northern Ireland. The President invited Boland to Áras an Uachtaráin, where he asked him to withdraw the resignation. Boland complied, only to resign formally nine months later in the midst of the famous Arms Crisis, during which the Taoiseach, Jack Lynch, called on the President to perform the unpleasant task of dismissing two senior ministers, Charles J. Haughey and Neil T. Blaney, for alleged gun running to Northern Ireland. The Taoiseach also hoped that de Valera would denounce the Provisional IRA's military campaign, but that denunciation was not forthcoming. 'I think,' Lynch explained afterwards, 'he felt that it wasn't for him at the end of his life to do so.'[35]

Any such pronouncement would probably have been resented even in some Fianna Fáil quarters. As it was, the President's failure to dissociate himself from the Lynch government in the aftermath of the Arms Crisis had already led to a certain amount of disillusionment. Both Kevin Boland and his father, Gerald, one of the last surviving members of the first Fianna Fáil government, were particularly disappointed, and their relations with the President cooled distinctly as a result. It was sad because the President obviously retained a good deal of respect and affection for the older Boland, as was evidenced following the latter's death in 1971. While paying his last respects at the Boland home, de Valera leaned across the corpse and broke down sobbing.[36]

Although obviously a somewhat lonely man who had outlived most of his contemporaries, the President was the essence of composure on public and state occasions. Reviewing a guard of honour, he would do a magnificent job of overcoming his blindness by walking in step with his aide-de-camp. He also welcomed a great many people to Áras an Uachtaráin throughout his second term. In addition to such foreign dignitaries as President Richard M. Nixon of the United States, King Baudouin of the Belgians, and former President Charles de Gaulle of France, there were journalists, television personalities, and descendents of old friends. With those with whom he was able to relax, he would produce a bottle of whiskey from his desk and, notwithstanding his reputation as a non-drinker, would pour drinks for his guests and himself. Then that charm, so often lost behind his austere public image would blossom forth, and he would reveal himself an excellent conversationalist with a keen sense of humour.

Proscribed by the constitution from seeking a third term, de Valera — then in his ninety-second year — retired in 1973 and moved into a nursing home in the Dublin suburbs, where he died on 29 August 1975 after a short illness.

In the days immediately following his death, his career was widely assessed. For some people he had become the personification of Irish freedom and independence, while others took a harsher view. 'One can only look on Eamon de Valera's life as a failure,' the columnist Con Houlihan wrote. 'By his own stated ambitions he was a failure — it is as cruelly simple as that.'

De Valera had repeatedly stated that his two main ambitions were the revival of the Gaelic language and the ending of partition. Neither of those seemed even remotely near realisation at the time of his death. No doubt a much greater proportion of the Irish people had acquired a knowledge of the language over the years, but the proportion using it in their daily lives had unquestionably declined as Gaeltacht areas disappeared. Yet there was probably little or nothing

[148] more that he could have done to secure the realisation of that dream.

On the partition question, on the other hand, de Valera's record was definitely tarnished, as he had on occasions resorted to sheer demagoguery. He was certainly less than forthright during the Treaty negotiations of 1921 in seeking to use the Ulster issue as a pretext for breaking off the talks when the real stumbling block was the association question. He had already advocated in the Dáil that Ulster unionists should be allowed to vote themselves out of the Irish Republic, once it had been recognised. Subsequently he actually incorporated provisions in his alternative to the Treaty that were virtually identical with the Treaty's partition clauses. But he later exploited the partition issue to cover up the fact that the difference between the Treaty and what he wanted was only a 'little sentimental thing'. He managed to create the mistaken impression that the controversy that led to the Civil War had revolved around partition. For a time he even seemed to ape Adolf Hitler in trying to secure a Munich-like settlement of the question.

De Valera concentrated on anti-partitionism to the extent of neglecting reconciliation with Northern unionists. 'For every step we moved towards them,' he once told the Dáil, 'you know perfectly well they would regard it as a sign that we would move another, and they would not be satisfied, in my opinion, unless we went back and accepted the old United Kingdom, a common parliament for the two countries.' He really adopted his own variant of their policy of 'not an inch.' He was not even willing to take steps that would eliminate that discrimination in the twenty-six counties against Protestant values which provoked fears among Unionists that they would be discriminated against in a united Ireland. His unwillingness to act in that regard prompted the suspicion that he wanted to provoke a situation in which the only solution to partition would be the transfer of Northern Protestants to Britain. That suspicion was probably exaggerated, but it was still unfitting that he — the son of emigrants and the leader of a people who had for so long depended on emigration — should suggest a settlement that would compel the expulsion of the descendants of people who had, in effect, emigrated to Ireland more than three centuries earlier. However, during his final years in politics, he did abandon his demagogic approach to emphasise what he had recognised as early as 1921, that partition could not — and indeed should not, even if it could — be ended by force. When the IRA resorted to violence in the 1950s, his government re-introduced internment and thereby quickly undermined the campaign.

It was his earlier attitude towards the IRA that was basically responsible for the controversy that surrounded de Valera throughout his political career. In 1922 he really disagreed with the tactics of the faction of the organisation that occupied the Four Courts, but he refused to denounce them or to use his enormous influence in an effort to quieten the passions that were leading to civil strife. Indeed he can be held responsible for exciting those passions by referring recklessly to 'rights which a minority may justly uphold, even by arms against a majority'. During the Civil War he so vociferously supported the IRA that he helped to create the impression that he was one of its actual leaders. As a result he incurred the underlying enmity of supporters of the 1921 Treaty who held him primarily responsible for the Civil War. In the ensuing bitterness, people on both sides lost sight of the fact that the difference between de Valera and his opponents had only been over a 'little sentiment thing'. When he subsequently adopted the 'stepping-stone' approach advocated by his opponents, they actually opposed him. They had become so embittered by the events of the Civil War that they, in effect, forgot what they had been fighting for. Ironically, therefore, it was not his critics, but de Valera himself, who proved that he had been wrong when he contended that the Treaty did not provide the means to achieve freedom. His tragic failure to recognise the actual potential of the Treaty back in 1921 was probably the most serious blemish on his record, because that whole controversy was to be the single most divisive factor in Irish politics. In fact, the difference between the two main political parties throughout the remainder of de Valera's political career can be attributed to the split over the Treaty.

It would be wrong, however, to judge de Valera's career simply in the light of his tragic mistakes of 1922, or his failure to achieve his main ambitions, because he did have some very significant accomplishments. He had helped to end the Civil War and he did much to stabilise Irish society in the 1930s by the magnanimous way in which he accepted and worked with prominent civil servants who had not only been appointed by his Civil War opponents but also undoubtedly shared their outlook. In addition, he did much to take the gun out of Irish politics both by his courageous response to those resorting to force and also by removing an emotive grievance through his demonstration to the Irish people — and to the whole world — that the twenty-six counties constituted a politically independent country.

In fairness to W. T. Cosgrave and his colleagues, it should be noted that they tried hard to demonstrate that independence themselves. And they were successful to a degree, both in getting the country elected to the Council of the League of Nations and in helping to secure the Statute of Westminster. But it was de Valera who was able to make the most of those two achievements. Using the Statute of Westminster, he managed to dismantle most of the disagreeable aspects of the 1921 Treaty. At the same time, he pursued a policy in the League of Nations that was not only [151] independent, but courageously so, especially during the Manchurian and Ethiopian crises when he did what he could to ensure that the League would be an effective force for peace. Foreseeing another major war after the League reneged on its responsibility to tackle the Ethiopian crisis effectively, de Valera abandoned his internationalist policy to adopt an isolationist approach.

In view of his courageous stands — in marked contrast to the timidity of the major democratic powers during the Manchurian and Ethiopian crises — de Valera and his government had absolutely nothing to be ashamed about in remaining neutral during the Second World War. And his successful struggle to keep Ireland out of that conflict in the face of IRA treachery, Allied pressure and Axis provocation was a magnificent achievement which provided the most conclusive demonstration of the country's political independence. It was, therefore, understandable that so many people should come to look on Eamon de Valera as the personification of Irish independence.

SUGGESTED FURTHER READING
Dwane, David T., *The Early Life of Eamon de Valera*, Dublin 1922.
Gwynn, Denis, *De Valera*, London 1933.
Longford, Earl of, and O'Neill, Thomas, *Eamon de Valera*, Dublin 1970.
MacManus, M. J., *Eamon de Valera*, Dublin 1957.
Moynihan, Maurice, ed., *Speeches and Statements by Eamon de Valera, 1917–73*, Dublin 1980.
Ó Faoláin, Seán, *De Valera*, London 1939.
O'Neill, T. P. and Ó Fiannachra, Padraig, *De Valera*, 2 vols, Dublin 1968–70.

Notes

Unfortunately Eamon de Valera's papers have not yet been released, but some individuals were given access to them before his death. The Earl of Longford and Thomas O'Neill have quoted liberally from those papers in their quasi-official biography, *Eamon de Valera*, which is an invaluable source of information, though it certainly could not be described as totally objective, nor could the multi-volume biography in Gaelic in which O'Neill and Padraig Ó Fiannachra are co-operating. The first two volumes, which cover up to 1938, really amount to an extended version of the Longford and O'Neill book, with a good deal of additional material quoted from de Valera's personal papers. Another with access to those papers, Maurice Moynihan, has edited an extensive compilation of de Valera's speeches and public statements.

For the earlier chapters I had access to a wealth of material at the State Paper Office in Dublin Castle. That material included de Valera's correspondence with Griffith both during his American mission (DE 2/245) and during the Treaty negotiations (DE 2/304). Additional letters from de Valera relating to the period were found in the papers of J. J. Hearne, James O'Mara and Joseph McGarrity in the National Library of Ireland. The extensive quotations from de Valera's civil war correspondence in the Longford-O'Neill biography are supplemented by his captured correspondence that was published at the time.

Some material relating to Anglo-Irish negotiations in regard to the oath and land annuities dispute is also in the State Paper Office (S. 6928). This is supplemented by Ronan Fanning's mammoth study, *The Irish Department of Finance*, for which he had access to material that is still classified. Also invaluable was David Harkness's excellent article, 'Mr de Valera's Dominion', which was based on British government documents, as was Deidre McMahon's UCD thesis, 'Malcolm MacDonald and Anglo-Irish Relations', which provides very useful information on events leading to the Anglo-Irish agreements of 1938. Joseph Connolly's unpublished 'Memoirs' provides a valuable insight into de Valera at the League of Nations, as does Stephen A. Barcroft's TCD thesis, 'The International Civil Servant'.

For the material on the years covering the Second World War I have relied mainly on earlier research for my *Irish Neutrality and the USA*, which depended heavily on United States and Canadian diplomatic documents, while Joseph T.

Carroll's *Ireland in the War Years* relied on British documents, and Carolle J. Carter made extensive use of German diplomatic papers for her book, *The Shamrock and the Swastika*. The final chapter is heavily dependent on contemporary press reports. In view of the nature of this study I have tried to keep actual footnotes to an absolute minimum. The following relate to material that might otherwise be considered controversial.

[153]

1. Longford and O'Neill, *De Valera*, 46.
2. de V. to Griffith, 9/7/19.
3. de V., speech at Bellevue-Stratford Hotel, Philadelphia, 1/10/19, Philadelphia *Public Ledger*, 2/10/19.
4. de V. to Griffith, 25/3/20.
5. de V. to Griffith, 10/3/20.
6. de V. to Griffith, 17/2/20.
7. de V. to Griffith, 6/3/20.
8. de V. to Griffith, 10/3/20.
9. de V. to Griffith, 25/3/20.
10. *Ibid.*
11. de V. to Griffith, 6/3/20.
12. O'Kelly to de V., 17/4/21.
13. de V. to Boland, quoted in Boland to O'Mara, 29/3/21, James O'Mara Papers, NLI.
14. Lloyd George to King George V, 21/7/21, Nicolson, *King George V*, 357.
15. Dáil Éireann, *Private Sessions*, 29.
16. de V. to McGarrity, 27/12/21, McGarrity Papers, NLI.
17. *Ibid.* 18. *Ibid.*
19. de V. to Griffith, 14/10/21.
20. Dáil Éireann, *Private Sessions*, 186.
21. *Ibid.*, 137. 22. *Ibid*
23. *Ibid.*, 153. 24. *Ibid.*
25. *Ibid.*, 123.
26. de V. to Ó Murchada, 3/10/22.
27. de V., statement, 1/5/22.
28. de V. to McGarrity, 10/9/22.
29. de V. to Ó Murchada, 13/9/22.
30. *Ibid.*
31. Fionan Lynch to editor, *Kerryman*, 6/8/32.
32. Sir Thomas Inskip, memo. of conversation with de V., 8/9/38, in McMahon, 'Malcolm MacDonald and Anglo-Irish Relations', a UCD thesis.
33. Joseph Connelly, 'Memoirs', MS in private possession.
34. Smyllie to Mulcahy, 21/5/41, Mulcahy Papers, UCD.
35. RTE interview, 31/8/75.
36. Boland, *Up Dev.*, 17.

Index